LOBBYING
FOR
CHANGE

LOBBYING
FOR
CHANGE

FIND YOUR VOICE TO CREATE
A BETTER SOCIETY

ALBERTO ALEMANNO

ICON

Published in the UK in 2017
by Icon Books Ltd, Omnibus Business Centre,
39–41 North Road, London N7 9DP
email: info@iconbooks.com
www.iconbooks.com

Sold in the UK, Europe and Asia
by Faber & Faber Ltd, Bloomsbury House,
74–77 Great Russell Street,
London WC1B 3DA or their agents

Distributed in the UK, Europe and Asia
by Grantham Book Services, Trent Road, Grantham NG31 7XQ

Distributed in the USA
by Publishers Group West,
1700 Fourth Street, Berkeley, CA 94710

Distributed in Australia and New Zealand
by Allen & Unwin Pty Ltd,
PO Box 8500, 83 Alexander Street,
Crows Nest, NSW 2065

Distributed in South Africa
by Jonathan Ball, Office B4, The District,
41 Sir Lowry Road, Woodstock 7925

Distributed in India by Penguin Books India,
7th Floor, Infinity Tower – C, DLF Cyber City,
Gurgaon 122002, Haryana

Distributed in Canada by Publishers Group Canada,
76 Stafford Street, Unit 300
Toronto, Ontario M6J 2S1

ISBN: 978-178578-285-5

Typeset in Minion by Marie Doherty

Printed and bound in the UK by Clays Ltd, St Ives plc

To my girls,
Mariana, Marianita, Isabella and Allegra Alemanno,
who make me smile every day
and remind me how beautiful life is.

Contents

Acknowledgements

When I began working on this book two years ago, the case for citizen lobbying was incipient, yet not clear. Had the book been published at that time it would have been both premature and prescient. Today lobbying for change appears to be an urgent and salient necessity. Amid a rapid acceleration of the political narratives and an ongoing transformation of economic and social agendas across liberal democracies, a citizen awakening has indisputably occurred. Millions of citizens across the world are becoming increasingly aware of their own collaborative power. This book is firstly dedicated to them.

This book would have never seen the light of day without the generous and inspiring contribution of many people who expressed interest in my ideas and work over the years. I am extremely grateful to my own institution HEC Paris, in particular the HEC Foundation and Labex Ecodec, as well as NYU School of Law, for the support received over the years and for letting me experiment with new forms of teaching and engaged scholarship. Thanks to HEC I was able to pioneer mass online teaching, by first making all my recorded classes freely available on iTunes and, second, by designing a Massive Open Online Course on Coursera. As a result, I reached out to more than 200,000 people around the globe. While I could not meaningfully engage with all of them (their figure is higher than the total number of students I will be meeting in my entire academic career), I have had the opportunity to meet many of them, often serendipitously (in the Paris metro, at airports and conferences), and learn from them. I can't image a more rewarding teaching and human experience. Thanks to NYU School of Law I was able to set up the EU Public Interest Clinic which has served dozens of civil society organisations while training a new generation of public interest lawyers. My students have been an excellent early audience, attentive and receptive, often critical of many of the views exposed in this book.

Several other audiences, from Tokyo University (where I teach every October on the Master's in Public Policy programme) and St. Gallen University (where I've designed the Lobbying & Advocacy module), to the participants in the EU Pro Bono Masterclasses we offer across Europe, also provided useful feedback.

From the very first moment we met, Kiera Jamison was a dream editor: patient and wise. She believed in my project from day one! Thank you to Andrew Furlow and his team at Icon Books for a smooth publication ride as well as to my publicist Ruth Killick.

I was lucky enough to receive advice and feedback from a close group of trusted friends: Alessandro Spina, Gianluca Sgueo, Helen Darbishire, Bing Taylor, Andras Baneth, Rosana Plaza, Benjamin Bodson, Igor Celikovic, Anne-Lise Sibony, Cliff Wirajendi, Leandro Machado, Ana Benje, Ailish Campbell, Jo Sparber and Yacine Kouhen. I've also benefited from advice and exchanges with Slav Todorov, Amandine Garde (Liverpool University), Daniel Freund (Transparency

International EU), Mariella Palazzolo (Telos), Lisa Witter (Apolitico), Aidan O'Sullivan (EU Ombudsman), Cinzia Ansaldi, Heather Grabbe and Neil Campbell (Open Society), Cinzia Seccamani, Xavier Dutoit (We Move), Liz Hamburg (Taproot Foundation), Vesco Paskalev (Hull University), Laurent Pech (Middlesex University), Vigjilenca Abazi (Maastricht University) and the Riparte il Futuro's team, in particular Federico Anghelé and Mattia Ansaldi.

A special thanks goes to the community of Young Global Leaders of the World Economic Forum. Becoming a part of YGL has had a profound yet subtle change in my world views. It not only broadened my horizons and brought special friendships into my life, but also inspired and strengthened me to do more to bring positive change into the world.

Thanks must also go to Charlelie Jourdan and Gauthier Bas from Old Continent for the fruitful cooperation and mutual learning over the years. I am also grateful to Ros Taylor, Lucien Midot, Nick Jones and Alexander Preter for research and editorial assistance.

Finally, thanks to the extraordinarily talented and dedicated team at The Good Lobby. I am particularly grateful to my colleague and friend Lamin Khadar for believing in creating a community of citizen lobbyists together, as well as to our colleagues and friends Ana Benje, Alexandre Biard, Andrea Boccuni, Giacomo Delinavelli, Barbara Holzer, Rosana Plaza, Simona Pronckute, Thais Rivera, Jéremy Charles, Roberto Tomasi, David Fernandez Rojo, Irina Lysenko, Andrea Tittelova and the many others who are joining our community.

Muchas gracias to my girls – my wife Mariana and my daughters Marianita, Isabella and Allegra – who make me smile and remind me daily how beautiful life is. And that is despite the many flights and the hours, days, weeks and months I spend in front of my computer, reading and writing instead of being with them. Another special *grazie* goes to my parents, Gianfranco and Biancamaria, who not only shared their youth with me and my sister Micol but – whether deliberately or not – offered me the best possible education to become first a citizen, and then a citizen lobbyist.

'It is not enough to be busy. So are the ants.
The question is: What are we busy about?'
Henry David Thoreau

'We do not need magic to change the world.
We carry all the power we need inside ourselves
already: we have the power to imagine better.'
J.K. Rowling

Introduction

If you're anything like me, you are probably unhappy with the way the world and our societies are working. And with good reason.

We, citizens living in democratic societies, are richer, safer, live longer and respect each other's rights more than ever before, yet we tolerate daily injustice and growing inequality.

We have talents, expertise and plenty of 'friends' (and we exchange thoughts and images with them daily on social media), yet we mobilise them not to improve the lives of the less privileged, but to make our own lives marginally more comfortable.

We have the right to vote for our representatives, and have never enjoyed (at least on paper) so many opportunities to participate directly in local and national affairs, yet our voices go mostly unheard. This may be surprising to some, but there are many more avenues for participation across liberal democracies than we are generally aware of.[1] In the US, three-quarters of all cities have developed opportunities for citizen involvement in strategic planning. The EU has also created many channels of public participation, but they remain little known and largely underused.[2] The World Bank has invested $85 billion over the last decade to support community participation worldwide.

We have never been in a better position to improve our communities and the world, yet we feel increasingly powerless to do so. Amid ubiquitous market and government surveillance, which is driven by unaccountable algorithms, we are increasingly made powerless by design.

The internet has enhanced our democracy, by ensuring greater access to information and fewer obstacles to connect with each other. Yet our digital social existence has turned into a echo chamber, where we discuss similar views with like-minded peers and fail to penetrate other social bubbles that are often misled by fear and xenophobia.[3]

As as an academic in his ivory tower, any question about the actual impact of my daily work makes me nervous. On average, only one in twenty students retains what they learn in one of my lectures.[4] When it comes to my research, the average scientific article is read by only ten people (who are generally colleagues).[5] But think about it: in your day job, how much of a positive impact do you have on the lives of others? If you are a nurse, a doctor, a schoolteacher or perhaps a committed politician then the answer is likely to be 'a lot', but most of us have limited scope to contribute to society through our daily jobs. Isn't that a paradox? The more professional a society becomes, the less it takes advantage of its own skills. It doesn't really matter whether you are a student, a jobseeker, a professional, an entrepreneur, an artist or a plumber: beyond the contributions we make to our company or organisation, we fail to harness our potential to benefit society. Sometimes we don't even know what our talents are. (Do you? Don't worry if not. If you look for one, you will find it!)

Our education systems, our jobs and our societies limit our ability to put our expertise and talents to use for the good of all. Instead, we outsource problems to our elected political representatives and big corporations who cheerfully decide what's best for us. No wonder elected officials and the market largely ignore citizens' opinions in favour of affluent and well-connected lobbyists.

We feel stuck. And we really *are* stuck, both as individuals and as a society, as we retreat into ever-smaller circles of 'friends', 'likers' and 'followers' within which we feel in control. Meanwhile, we have grown more cynical about the value of democracy as a political system and have become less hopeful that anything we do might influence public policy.[6] As a result, we're failing to take meaningful, collective action on issues that are threatening our future and already shaping our lives, such as climate change, migration flows, the technological revolution or the rising tide of populism.[7] Every day that we don't act, the problem gets worse. We seem to grasp this, but we carry on being helpless bystanders.

Let's admit it: we live in societies paralysed by widespread frustration. Complacency keeps us locked into the system. Instead of harnessing our talents to better society, we drift passively through our lives in the same way that we swipe a mobile phone screen. Often, the two activities are indistinguishable. Every time we are confronted with an opportunity to engage that might disrupt our daily routine, we ask ourselves the same self-absorbed questions. What's in it for me? Can I put it on my CV? Will it help get me a job, or improve my life? Will my action really make a difference?

We are spectators, not actors. Consumers, not citizens.

Yet having control over our lives is one of the essential

elements of well-being.[8] Aristotle, nearly two and a half millennia ago, believed happiness was not just a feeling, but a practice, which he called *eudaemonia*. Contemporary research into happiness has borne him out: people who participate in and contribute to public life are more satisfied with their personal lives.[9] This is not necessarily because they get exactly what they want, but because taking part releases feelings of autonomy, competence and social connectedness. As the Nobel prize-winner Amartya Sen has argued, helping to shape the decisions that affect your own life and other peoples' is fundamental to human well-being.[10]

And more than that – when you compare it with other indicators of well-being like wealth or education – participation in public life has one of the greatest effects on long-term happiness.[11] This is because when you do it you forge personal connections and – together – you help others, fostering a joint sense of purpose. The more you participate in public life, the more fulfilled you will be. The effect is not just psychological, either. People who engage with public life tend to enjoy longer, healthier lives.[12] Conversely, citizens who feel estranged from society might become culturally homeless – they do not connect or belong to the local culture nor to that of another nation. As such, they are typically unhappy and often attracted to extremist positions. Indeed, research shows that the psychological need for significance, not religion or ideology, is what propels people toward extremism.[13]

We often 'like' good causes on Facebook. Sometimes we even sign a petition on campaigning platforms like Avaaz. Once in a while we might donate to international charities like

Save the Children, Oxfam or Action Aid. Perhaps we give a few coins to a beggar. Some of you might have even contributed to a crowdfunded campaign on platforms like Indiegogo or Kickstarter (if not, check them out!) for a good cause.

Let's be honest: while these easy forms of engagement may make us feel better about ourselves and perform some virtue-signalling, they are always going to be inadequate.

First, we're not the ones who chose the cause, let alone who come up with a solution. We've resigned ourselves to buying into ready-made campaigns. Even taking these small steps leaves us as spectators rather than actors.

Second, by offering things that require so little effort – a signature, a second of our spare time, some change or second-hand items – we fail to really engage and share a part of ourselves. Our contribution engages us as atomised individuals who sign and/or donate, not as community members.

Third, we all have skills, talents and expertise to offer, but these ready-made campaigns and activities don't give us any opportunity to put them to use.

One-click participation should be the beginning, not the end of our engagement. Don't get me wrong: supporting valuable campaigns is great, but it falls way short of bringing your own experience, skills and ideas to these battles. Trust me: you have so much more to give.

Let's assume that you would be ready to give some of your time, talent and expertise – or even devote part of your life – to fix one issue you feel deeply passionate about. You feel discriminated against because of your sexual orientation.

Maybe you worry about finding a job (or the job you want). Your elderly mother or grandmother needs professional care and she isn't getting it. You hate that the beautiful square where you live is full of parked cars. You want cheaper kindergartens for your kids. You wish the local Roman Catholic church could be used for Muslim rituals, too. You would like the animals you eat to lead better lives. You want to spend less time on your tax return.

Or, on a bigger scale, you might have ideas about how to reform the job market, to promote LGBT rights, to improve the healthcare system or local transport, schools, religious freedom, animal welfare or the taxation system. Most of the time you probably feel it's not even worth trying to change things. But suspend your doubts for a moment. Let's assume you are going to give it a try.

Where to Begin?

Given the widespread belief that businesses run the world – symbolised by the current allure of the Silicon Valley start-up scene – it's tempting to conclude that you need to set up a company in order to change society. It would most likely be a social enterprise, which would contribute toward addressing any of the challenges I've just mentioned. It might also make you rich and famous. Maybe it would even turn you into a philanthropist. Yet we often forget that businesses, just like ourselves, operate (or at least ought to) within the boundaries set out by government.[14]

Government, not businesses, shapes our individual and collective chances of success in life: it determines vital issues like access to education, healthcare and, consequently, life expectancy. It does this by laying down the 'rules of the game' – the public policies governing our daily actions, which should in turn reflect our collective preferences. So we should expect government to set emission standards for cars, to regulate the safety of the prescribed drugs we take or the market for cannabis for recreational uses, and to determine road safety rules. Likewise, despite all the talk of corporate social responsibility, evidence suggests that it is public policy – the means by which a government addresses the needs of its citizens – that usually pushes an entire industry to embrace a new business model.[15] As argued by Manuel Arriaga, policy-driven action reboots the system by creating a new, irreversible best practice.[16]

Like it or not, governments are the only institutions that truly represent us – our wishes, rights and aspirations. They hold the keys to change. Even as people's political apathy and disaffection grow, this is still true.[17] Only a few individuals in society tend to devote time to the political process (and I don't blame you for not being among them!), but *everyone* is affected by the policies it makes.

So, even though businesses make huge contributions to society, we had better start with government action if we want to make the world a better place.[18] And at a time of increasing disaffection with politics, our elected representatives need us more than ever (though they might not always be aware of it). Shrinking water supplies, 65 million people displaced across the world,[19] the disruption brought about by the fourth industrial revolution on our way of life:[20] these are challenges they can't tackle adequately without the public's help.

This might seem too ambitious. But telling your elected representatives what you think they should do, and whether they're doing it properly – and to do so in ways beyond simply signing online petitions – could be the most effective way to put an end to our individual and collective feeling of powerlessness. You can change their priorities and influence how they design and develop policies – whether on pensions, unemployment, environmental protection, migration reform and so on.

I'm not advising you to go into politics (though if you want to, please go ahead – we need capable people!). But if you want to have an impact (rather than just talking about the issues) *not* being a full-time politician might even be to your advantage, given our widespread disenchantment and growing distrust of political parties.[21] Politicians sometimes seem to spend more time honing their personal images than doing their jobs, and our political leaders often seem to dump their long-term policy ideals in favour of winning elections.[22]

This crisis in trust is paving the way for a remarkable, yet largely unnoticed, split between the world of politics and the world of policy. Politics is the realm of a small, self-referential elite. Dominated by a party-based network of public speakers, its aim is to leave a positive yet short-lived impression on you. Policy, on the other hand, has become an ever-expanding, accessible and inclusive world, inhabited by a panoply of actors – ranging from policy analysts, journalists, activists, think-tankers, civil servants and civic entrepreneurs to a few, exceptionally committed politicians who do their jobs well. It's a demanding environment with little room for improvisation, and where, increasingly, evidence matters more than ideology.

Joining a political party demands compromise and loyalty. So it's hardly surprising that political parties increasingly struggle to identify and recruit talented candidates. On the other hand, the worlds of policy and government business attract more and more 'wonks' whose relevance and impact grow daily. They're outnumbering politicians. That's where the power game really is. That's the apolitical[23] world this book will show you how to navigate.

Now we've identified where change takes place – the world of policy as opposed to the world of politics – the next step is to make sure that change will actually happen. After that, we just need to learn how to bring about change.

If you picked up this book, you are likely to be relatively young – or at least youthfully optimistic. You are likely to be someone who cares and believes that it is still possible to shift from 'me' to 'we' in order to change the world.

But what if you're neither young nor a believer that change is possible? I hope to persuade you that there are very good reasons to believe it, and in this book I will show plenty of evidence that you, as an individual, can help to solve many of the problems affecting your community and the world, without ever running for election.

Paralysed by the hyperactivity of our daily lives, devalued by the educational system and bamboozled by the arrogant rhetoric of many politicians, we are discouraged from believing that ordinary citizens have a role to play in changing the status quo. Today businesses and governments have ever more data about us and know how to use it, yet we citizens know next to nothing about what they are doing with it.[24] This imbalance of information control and use is not only an issue of power, but also one of rights and dignity. Yet because we think our voices don't matter, it seems to make little difference who's in charge. In any case, we lack a reason to get involved. Again, what's in it for us?

This has been the case for a long time. But one thing has changed. The information and digital revolution is shaking the foundations of the status quo as we know it, opening up an array of ways to influence how policies are made.[25] Digital technology has already created more opportunities for more people than any technological change since the printing press.[26] Google, Facebook, Twitter, Snapchat, Instagram and Tumblr are radically changing how ideas spread, influence others and create networks and communities of change. While their democratising potential must not be overrated,[27] their mere existence suggests that there has never been a better time for citizens to have their say and organise.

In our socially networked societies, the publication of one document on WikiLeaks may redefine international relations. Revolutions – like the Arab Spring – can be kicked off via social media. One wrong step online can put you out of business and make you unemployable. When a money manager shared false investment information via tweets and email to a list of 60,000 people, he was fined $100,000 by the US Securities and Exchange Commission. We are the first generation with direct, unmediated access to the world.[28] Technology can act as a great social equaliser. It puts resources formerly available to the few in the hands of the many.[29] If we are no longer content to be spectators, we can become actors. If we are no longer content to be consumers, we can become citizens, again. As Dorothy Cotton sang during the US civil rights movement, 'We are the Ones We've Been Waiting for'. Millions of citizens across the world are becoming increasingly aware of their own collaborative power.

But how do we convert digital attention into meaningful action? How can you realistically accommodate new forms of participation and engagement into your busy daily routine? How do you channel the new-found exuberance and promise of this technological empowerment into your own life?

According to received wisdom, there are two main ways of taking part in a democracy. Firstly, you can vote. Casting your ballot for local or national representatives supports a given political agenda. You can also volunteer for – or donate to – political campaigns, by canvassing door-to-door, holding public meetings, raising money and helping attract media coverage.

Voting is the most familiar and widely touted form of citizen participation. Many of us have a wide range of elected officials we can vote for, at the local, regional, national and even international level. Voting matters, and we should all take part. The other way of participating is to run for office. You need a political party to co-opt you (a bit like joining a tribe), then support you. Never forget, you must then accept the rules that govern the electoral game. Good luck.

But there are limitations to both these forms of participation.

Voting is undergoing a profound crisis. Elections are occasional events with limited choices, and turnout is not only low but also falling in most countries – particularly among young people. We'll look at this in more detail in Part I of the book.

While political parties have historically guaranteed the citizen-democracy connection, they are facing dramatic decline – not only in membership, but also in their popular appeal and endorsement. Rather than promoting democratic renewal, outmoded party machines are making it more difficult. Hence the countless calls for more 'direct democracy' – a system in which people choose policy initiatives directly – in our system of government. Yet, as Podemos in Spain, the Five Star Movement in Italy, the various Pirate parties and many other protest movements have shown, 'direct democracy' is not in itself a viable response to many of society's challenges. First, these self-proclaimed, technology-enabled experiences of direct democracy haven't succeeded in meaningfully engaging their followers.[30] Second, experience both in parliament and in local government confirms that protest parties railing against 'the system' are as likely to find themselves being absorbed by it as they are to transform it once in office. Third, Facebook-type networks are great for gathering people at protests, but not for building stable political organisations.[31] At the time of writing, both Podemos and the Five Star Movement are undergoing internal fights threatening their existence.

There is a growing need for alternative, unconventional forms of participation that can reconnect the elected representatives with the public. Voting and running for office isn't enough; social media networks aren't enough. There's an alternative space to be filled in today's (representative) democracies.

Fortunately, there is also a third, less well-known way to make a difference in public life: lobbying. Don't recoil at the word! Although you may previously have only heard about lobby groups that represent the interests of big business, whether that's the pharmaceutical industries or big tobacco companies, it is possible to lobby for good. Lobbying may be the second-oldest profession on the planet, and it is probably the most widely misunderstood (and misused) phenomenon surrounding the healthy functioning of government and society.

Lobbying enables anyone to engage with the policy process directly, by influencing elected representatives to initiate – or block – a given policy, whether it's fracking, LGBT rights, or reforming the pension system. It involves writing to policy-makers to influence them, arranging meetings with politicians or pressuring them into taking a particular course of action, but also mobilising other citizens, building alliances and conveying information to both decision-makers and the public. Thanks to the digital revolution and a myriad of new channels of participation, lobbying has never been so easy.

Contrary to conventional wisdom, lobbying is not only legitimate but also necessary – provided that everyone (including you) has the chance to get involved, which hasn't always been the case. It ensures citizens and interest groups are directly represented in the policy process by circumventing the traditional, often insidious and oligarchic, channels of political representation. Lobbying empowers you and your community. You may end up being surprised and delighted by how much difference you can make.

But Why Should *You* Become a Lobbyist?

You have a busy life and certainly better things to do than to spend time with politicians (unless you need their favour or you nurture some political ambitions). In real life, only citizens hired by a company such as Coca-Cola, Google or Toyota, or a non-profit organisation such as Greenpeace or Amnesty International; your city office or a trade union, agree to lobby on behalf of their clients. This is generally a full-time job that can be performed in-house (you're hired by Google, your city or Save the Children) or by an external consultant.

There are many more lobbyists in our societies than you might expect. Most of the time their work is not reflected by their job title. A CEO is also a lobbyist for her company's interest, insofar as she represents and defends that company in the public space. The same applies to a teacher working for her school, or an NGO activist volunteering for his organisation. The both speak on behalf of their institutions and promote their interests. Perhaps your job entails a lobbying task but you have never realised it. We all lobby, in our own way. That's what we are expected to do in a society where there are more and more interests to be taken into account.

Lobbying is a fact of public life in our democracies: lobbyists' jobs are advertised in newspapers, their position papers circulate in government and they advertise at bus stops (generally presented as 'public affairs' positions). Unfortunately organised interests, notably corporations, have historically monopolised (even hijacked) lobbying. On average, out of the 100 organisations that spend the most on lobbying in developed countries, 95 represent businesses.[32] Furthermore, many of the non-business organisations that claim to speak for citizens lack representation.[33] But these elements do not exhaust the possibilities of lobbying. Thanks to the information revolution and the opening-up of the policy process, lobbying is no longer the prerogative of well-funded groups with huge memberships and countless political connections. And that's what this book is about: democratising lobbying. We need more – not less – lobbying, but of a different kind: lobbying by the citizens, for the citizens.

To many, 'citizen lobbying' sounds like an oxymoron. And so it is, if you believe that lobbyists represent – by definition – the interests of some rather than all, meaning they can never be a force for good. When I was still a conventional academic insulated in my comfortable ivory tower, I shared that belief. Now, after years of direct engagement in advocacy campaigns, I see it differently. Citizens and civil society organisations can lobby for good. So can corporations.[34] And sometimes all these actors can even team up to speed up change.[35] Imagine the corporate world lobbying together for decisive and effective action to curb climate change, or to promote fair pay. The best lobbyists, marketers, strategists, all mobilised as one for a good cause… Imagine if the non-profit world enjoyed the same resources and expertise as the corporate world. This is the goal pursued by my organisation, The Good Lobby, an advocacy skill-sharing community connecting real people – citizen experts, such as academics and professionals as well as job-seekers and students – with civil society organisations who work on the most important public issues.[36]

My first experience of citizen lobbying came in 2009. I was teaching a class in Paris to a crowd of students from all over the world. I wanted to illustrate to my students how they – as citizens who knew little or nothing about lobbying – could make a difference by winning a major battle for millions of consumers.

I asked them what they thought of international roaming charges. These are the extra fees mobile operators apply when we make calls from abroad. Being deliberately provocative, I suggested roaming charges should be eliminated as they hampered our freedom of movement, thereby limiting economic and personal freedom across European countries. Only a few weeks after that class, thanks to the entrepreneurship and commitment of a former student of mine, I found myself involved in one of the first popular petitions ever lodged in the EU. In fact, it was one of the first European Citizens' Initiatives (ECI) ever submitted. An ECI is a transnational petition system that enables citizens of at least seven different European countries to start collecting the 1 million signatures required to prompt the EU to adopt a new policy. Although we never managed to collect that many signatures, we set in motion an EU-wide public debate – through a low-cost, social media-powered marketing campaign. It led the former Competition Commissioner Neelie Kroes to propose the abolition of international roaming charges to the European Parliament and EU governments. They will be gone by the end of 2017, to the benefit of more than 500 million citizens.

Success is relative. We failed to get the signatures we needed but we brought about a systemic change. And we did all of this without taking the credit. That's the essence of citizen lobbying: learning, testing and making things happen *within the system*. Since then I've been involved in dozens of citizen lobbying campaigns and trained hundreds of students, activists and professionals to become citizen lobbyists across the world. Here are a few more examples.

Alejandro Calvillo and his wife Elaine Kemp, who live in Mexico, launched a fight against sodas and their harmful effects on health. Mexicans are among the biggest consumers of drinks with added sugar. As a result, they have one of the highest rates of obesity and diabetes in the world. The poor are particularly affected, putting a heavy burden on Mexico's public health system.

Alejandro and Elaine decided to create an association to counter soda manufacturers' lobbying and ad campaigns, which claimed that physical activity mattered more than diet, despite the scientific evidence to the contrary. They called their association El Poder del Consumidor (Consumer Power). By organising street events and academic conferences, they gradually attracted people's attention. By 2012, Michael Bloomberg's foundation for public health was giving them enough funding to stand up to counter-attacks by the manufacturers and their tame politicians. Eventually, a bill was passed in 2014 which imposed a 'soda tax'.

Soda consumption fell by 17 per cent in a year. This piece of legislation has inspired other countries to consider following Mexico's example. Alejandro and Elaine are citizen lobbyists.

Sofia Ashraf is now an internationally acclaimed Indian Tamil rapper. But until December 2015, she was a creative supervisor at Ogilvy & Mather, a global advertising firm that counts Unilever among its clients. Sofia resigned from her job when she took up the cause of local workers' associations that had been seeking compensation from Unilever for 14 years. Unilever allegedly operated a thermometer plant in Tamil Nadu that spilt mercury into a local river, killing dozens and incapacitating others.

Sofia released a rap about the spill called 'Kodaikanal Won't!', denouncing Unilever. It went viral on YouTube. In 2016 Unilever finally agreed to compensate the victims for their losses in an out-of-court settlement. Thanks to Sofia, poisoned workers secured justice and the Jhatkaa association is now trying to ensure Unilever cleans up the river at its own expense. Sofia Ashraf is a citizen lobbyist.

Max Schrems, an Austrian law student, stood up to Facebook in 2013. After a short stay in California as an exchange student, he discovered that the company had circumvented the EU data protection regime when transferring his data (and those of millions of other Europeans) to the US. After crowdfunding his campaign, he succeeded in successfully challenging Facebook through the Irish authorities and eventually the EU Court of Justice.

Max epitomises citizen lobbying. He occupied the space left vacant by regulators, enforcers and civil society organisations. We need more Max Schrems in the world, and I hope he will inspire others. Max himself drew inspiration from Edward Snowden, another citizen lobbyist, whose whistle-blowing revealed the largest surveillance system ever deployed by a democratic country.

Jon Worth, a Briton who lives in Berlin, is a self-made campaigner who devotes his life to denouncing political abuses. He persistently spends hours every day monitoring – predominantly on Twitter – the action of many national and European members of parliament. He flags up their abuses, inconsistencies and acts in what he believes to be the public interest. Jon is a citizen lobbyist.

Mari Takenouchi has been an anti-nuclear activist since 1999. In 2011 she and her son were living near the Fukushima plant in Japan. Since then, as an independent journalist, she has been fighting – with the Save Kids Japan association – for recognition of the harmful effects even low-level radiation has on children. In 2014, she took to task a nuclear lobbyist and former Japanese premier on Twitter for encouraging locals to return to their homes near the crippled plant. She alleged that the Ethos group he was supporting, driven underground by the French nuclear multinational Areva, intended to conduct live experiments on humans. Mari has undergone several interrogations by the Japanese police and risks a prison sentence. Her case has attracted the attention of the international community and triggered several campaigns and petitions, notably by Reporters Without Borders. They have shone a light on the largely hidden links between nuclear lobbyists and the Japanese government. Mari is a citizen lobbyist.

Ben Goldacre, a brilliant British physician and academic, decided after years of serious research to start writing to sensitise the UK population to what he called 'bad science'. In 2012 he showed that a substantial proportion of medical research goes unpublished (estimates range from one-third to one-half). In particular, he highlighted that thousands of clinical trials have not reported their results; some have not even been registered. Information on what was done and what was found in these trials could be lost forever to doctors and researchers, leading to bad treatment decisions, missed opportunities for good medicine and trials being repeated. He has also shown that negative findings are less likely to be published than positive ones, even in the absence of conflicts of interest.

Against this backdrop, Ben launched AllTrials, a campaign countering the phenomenon of under-reporting of clinical trials and advocating that clinical research adopt the principles of open research. The project summarises itself as 'All trials registered, all results reported': that is, all clinical trials should be listed in a registry and their results should always be shared as open data. At the heart of the organisation is a petition signed by over 85,000 individuals and 599 organisations. Ben is a citizen lobbyist.

Regardless of whether you care about matters of general public interest, such as consumer and patient rights (like Sofia in India and Ben in the UK), data protection (like Max in Europe), environmental protection (like Mari in Japan), public health (like Alejandro and Elaine in Mexico), the accountability of our elected representatives (like Jon in the EU) or whether you care about people whose voices go unheard, turning yourself into a citizen lobbyist can empower you. It can empower anyone who wants to affect the way policy is decided.

You can have 'a say' and even make a positive difference to other people's lives as an individual, as an organisation or both. And, as these examples show, you don't have to become an expert or understand all the intricacies of the policymaking process to be a good lobbyist. You just need passion for your cause and the ability to communicate it. Hard facts will also help. Citizen lobbying is cheap, fulfilling and you can do it from anywhere in the world. Just pick your cause.

By providing a counterweight to special interests, citizen lobbyists can improve the quality of policymaking. In the same way, they can hold consumer and pressure groups to genuinely acting in the public interest. Citizen lobbying hones the quality of policymaking while giving all of us a chance to learn about how government works.

This book explores both the dark and light sides of lobbying as it is deployed by both professional lobbyists and citizens. And it shows how corporations can use lobbying to support and build on a commitment to trading responsibly. There's no reason why the right cause shouldn't unite citizens and corporations to work together to change policy.

Why This Book?

Building on my personal experience as educator, scholar and civic advocate, this book offers a guide to becoming an effective citizen lobbyist in your daily life. It proposes a 10-step strategy to make you comfortable with lobbying – and get you doing it!

This is not an academic book. This is a volume that aspires to reach a broader audience, and to inspire you. It is not intended to contribute to the academic debate per se, but instead to build upon the insights academic theory offers in order to nurture an entirely different discussion: how to persuade ourselves that the break with our daily routine is worth it. It even tells you how to do it.

These are the three main goals of this book:

1. To share and promote an innovative form of do-it-yourself citizenship aimed at empowering ordinary citizens at a time of unprecedented social, economic and political volatility.

2. To demystify and democratise lobbying as a legitimate and healthy component of the democratic process.

3. To inspire a new generation of advocates, activists and engaged citizens to get involved in the unfashionable world of government.

Regardless of where you come from and what you do in life, every one of us has the capacity to be an effective citizen lobbyist. We have boundless reserves of untapped talent, energy and knowledge. You will be amazed at what you can achieve once you start to make lobbying part of your life.

Lobbying for Change is a down-to-earth, practical guide that will enable you to engage with the things that matter to you and to make an immediate impact on the world around you. I hope you will – because by embracing citizen lobbying, you can breathe life back into democracy and empower yourself and your community.

Throughout the book, you will find three types of extra content to inform and inspire you:

TIP

These boxes contain useful tips that complement the guidance provided in the main text.

ACTIVITY

These boxes suggest activities for you to try out what you have learned.

STORY

These boxes contain real-life examples of successful (and unsuccessful) instances of citizen lobbying. They offer practical illustrations of the dos and don'ts when using the toolbox.

PART I

THE PROBLEM

Powerless

'The only thing necessary for the triumph
of evil is for good men to do nothing.'
Edmund Burke

Many of us feel like spectators nowadays. Regardless of where we come from and what we do in life, despite the wealth and opportunities our societies offer, we feel overwhelmed and hopeless in the face of mounting challenges. We have never enjoyed so many opportunities to have a say in shaping our democratic societies. Yet we feel too feeble and helpless to do anything about it. We don't always grasp why this is.

Powerlessness has a profound effect on our physiology and mental capacity.[1] It amplifies our response to stress which, in the long run, damages the brain. This in turn inhibits our ability to function and engage with the world. It damages our individual and collective well-being.[2]

Many factors can explain why we feel so powerless – including an intriguing bystander effect that reinforces inaction[3] – but four things, all of them interconnected, are central to it:

- *Nobody speaks for you:* the unequal distribution of power;

- *You're not in the club*: the distance between voters and decision-makers;

- *Nobody teaches you:* the disconnect between our schools and reality;

- *Somebody decides for you:* powerlessness by design.

We're about to look at these in more detail. The remaining parts of this book will tackle what we can do about them.

Nobody Speaks for You: the Unequal Distribution of Power

> 'The reality of political life is that the voice
> that shouts the loudest is the most likely to
> be heard, no matter how numerous the silent
> majority, no matter how just their cause.'
> Brian Stipelman[4]

How can you feel powerless in a democracy? Doesn't democracy mean that power belongs to the people? At least that's what we learn at school. World leaders assure us that it's so. They may even compare our modern democracies with the ideal of the first known democracy in Athens. The truth, however, is that during the fourth century BC, there were probably no more than 100,000 people belonging to citizen families in Athens. In other words, about 30,000 adult male citizens were entitled to vote in the assembly.[5] If we, like the Athenians, lived in a small community where everyone could discuss issues of common interest, better their understanding in public debates, identify and assess available options and their consequences and eventually reach an informed consensus on what to do (based on universal suffrage and by a majority of individual voting), then we too might have a 'true' democracy.

Unfortunately, there are too many of us to make that work, and the delegation of political power is a necessary (if minor) evil. Indeed, the original idea of democracy, as the Ancient Greeks conceived it, was soon adapted by the Greeks themselves into an indirect, representative system that, wittingly or unwittingly, disempowered citizens (so as to empower them through their representatives). That's what we call representative democracy.

The 19th-century English liberal philosopher John Stuart Mill explained it as:

> the participation should everywhere be as great as the general degree of improvement of the community will allow ... But since all cannot, in a community exceeding a single small town, participate personally in any but some very minor portions of the public business, it follows that the ideal type of a perfect government must be representative.[6]

Indeed, representative democracy is often considered a compromise which is forced on us by practical constraints. But there is another case for it.

It also tempers high emotion and the ensuing violence of the majority. That's why we entrust a few citizens – today's politicians – with the task of governing us in our countries' best interests.[7] That's why today our political power is limited to expressing a preference for a candidate (sometimes not even that, due to the electoral system) or a party, rather than taking a stance on every single issue.

Under the model of representative democracy, we decided to raise up a governing elite who should be able, as US President and founding father James Madison saw it:

> to refine and enlarge the public views, by passing them through the medium of a chosen body of citizens, whose wisdom may best discern the true interest of their country, and whose patriotism and love of justice will be least likely to sacrifice it to temporary or partial considerations. Under such a model, it may well happen that the public voice, pronounced by the representatives of the people, will be more consonant to the public good than if pronounced by the people themselves, convened for the purpose.[8]

This vision has spread over time across liberal democracies, from France to Austria, from Germany to Spain. As a result, decisions are distanced from everyday people and delegated to their representatives. In other words, we deliberately established a governing elite. So it is no surprise that a small group of professional politicians – rather than us – do most of the public speaking and take the decisions on issues of broad concern.[9] It sounds like a fair division of labour: our representatives take care of the big challenges, since they are best able to do so, and we can spend our lives focusing on our own concerns without having to give much thought to what is happening in our society. Despite some disgracefully bad outcomes, this system has worked reasonably well for the last couple of centuries.

But today, elections, which made democracy possible, are the fossil fuel of politics. After giving democracy 'a huge boost, now they cause colossal problems'.[10] Our role as citizens, limited to voting every few years, is frequently sidelined and usually cosmetic. We think of government as *them*, not us. The Austrian-born US economist, Joseph Schumpeter likened democracy to a free market mechanism where parties (firms) have to sell the electorate (customers) the best policy in order to win their votes.[11] In other words, political candidates compete for votes in the same way firms compete for customers. This procedural understanding of democracy, which is partly shared by philosophers such as Max Weber and Norberto Bobbio, seems to legitimise a situation in which people play a minimal role in political life. It speaks to a commodification of politics. But democracy can't be reduced to voting. Elections cannot be an end in themselves.

Delegating the workings of democracy made sense when communication and access to knowledge were limited. But it is completely out of touch with the way we interact with each other and learn today. Even as long ago as the 18th century, Jean-Jacques Rousseau observed:

> The people of England deceive themselves when they fancy they are free; they are so, in fact, only during the election of members of parliament; for, as soon as a new one is elected, they are again in chains, and are nothing.[12]

If democracy boils down to a method of choosing political leaders, there is no room for a community to emerge that can tell the elected what citizens are thinking. As predicted by Mill, 'Let a person have nothing to do for his country and he will not care for it'.[13]

Despite these powerful reminders, the centralised systems of authority we find in today's representative democracies not only accept but actually reward political passivity. The habit is institutionally and culturally encouraged in each of us. How so? As it has recently been proven, what determines our political behaviour, in particular voting, is group identity and party loyalty rather than our policy preferences.[14] This explains why elections typically fail to result in popular control of public policy. It's no wonder we feel powerless; the system is structured so that we can't vote on individual policy issues. We are not supposed to be in control.

But could it be any other way? Any system of government needs administrators to carry out decisions. We have busy lives, little interest in the technicalities of decision-making and limited mental bandwidth. Evidence confirms that ordinary citizens do no master the intricacies of political issues.[15] Yet we – citizens – are expected to hold accountable those we hired to represent us, through a set of *counterpower mechanisms*. Political philosopher Pierre Rosanvallon refers to them as 'counterdemocracy'.[16] This is the essence of representative democracy and its intrinsic division of labour between *them* and *us*: those who hold power do not exercise it, but delegate it to those who exercise it but do not hold it. This is the key (yet often neglected) distinction between sovereignty (us) and governance (them).

But in order to hold officials accountable, we need to know them, and how many of us know our elected officials at a local, state and – if you are an EU citizen – European level? Only a small minority. Fusion's Massive Millennial Survey showed that 77 per cent of 18- to 34-year-olds could not name one of their senators in the US.[17] Similarly, 75 per cent of Britons are unable to name their MP.[18] Worse, just one in ten can identify their local Member of the European Parliament, according to the *Guardian*.[19] Similar trends are found across the world.

In these circumstances, we shouldn't be surprised that most of our politicians are persistently indifferent to us – except, of course, at election time when they court us for our votes. They respond instead to the affluent and organised. And in doing so they give the impression that not all citizens deserve equal consideration.

Voting is supposed to equalise power: the wealthy and the poor all have one vote and should equally be offered the opportunity to voice their concerns. This conclusion flies in the face of today's democratic realities. In particular, the contrast with our online experience, where each of us can speak our mind and expect our views to be considered and acted upon, is stark. This disconnect between our digitally-enabled lives as consumers and the low-tech, offline world of politics is sharper than ever. While our model of representative democracy rests on the premise that the elected respond to our opinion and represent the public interest, the practice of political representation – as experienced by all of us – proves that wrong. Without an equal voice for every citizen, there cannot be equal consideration of interests. As a result, there is a widespread belief that our votes do not really matter. Martin Gilens of Princeton University recently confirmed this conclusion with compelling evidence that the opinions of the bottom 90 per cent of income earners in America have a 'statistically non-significant impact'. As a result, the preferences of economic elites, business interests and people who can afford lobbyists have 'far more independent impact upon policy change than the preferences of average citizens do'.[20] Other studies have demonstrated that the large majority of the population, in particular those on lower incomes, are effectively excluded from the political system. Their opinions are systematically ignored by the elected representatives, while the preferences of a tiny segment of the richest have overwhelming influence.[21]

The fundamental problem in this system is that one set of interests systematically overpowers the others. The most powerful players in the policy game are the wealthy, the educated and the well-connected. Partisan interests, notably but not exclusively corporate ones, have the most resources, skills and commitment to participate in the day-to-day workings of government. As a result, even in the most democratic countries, we, the citizens, have only limited impact on policy decisions. You probably live in a democracy. But how democratic really is it?

This situation of systemic unbalances in the representation of interests is expected to worsen. Runaway inequality has created a world where eight people own as much as the poorest half of the world's population, according to a 2017 study.[22] This number has fallen dramatically from 388 as recently as 2010, 80 in 2015 and 62 in 2016.[23] While just six of the 62 were women in 2016, the eight super-rich in 2017 are all men.

Billionaires who own the same wealth as half the world
And what transport they would fit on

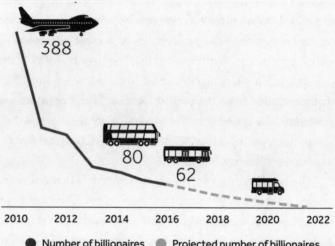

© Table – Oxfam, 2016[24]

Even if we accept – as we do – that lobbying is a legitimate activity aimed at informing the policy process by making sure everyone's interests are represented, policymakers hear far more from one side than from the other. While the evidence about the effectiveness of lobbying is mixed,[25] it is undeniable that having a louder voice improves your chance. More resources allow organised interests to hire more experienced and connected people, to work on more issues and to be more vocal.

In the 18th century, the Scottish moral philosopher and pioneer of political economy, Adam Smith, was already condemning the elite of his day – the 'merchants and manufacturers' of England. He identified them as 'the principal architects' of policy who strived to make sure that their own interests were 'most particularly attended to', even though the effect on others could be 'grievous'.

Today the scale of corporate lobbying is unprecedented. In the US, the $2.6 billion reportedly spent on it now adds up to more than the combined budgets of the Senate ($860 million) and the House of Representatives ($1.18 billion).[26] Business accounts for roughly 90 per cent of all reported lobbying expenditure in the EU.[27] As a result, 75 per cent of declared lobbying meetings between EU lobbyists and public authorities in the first half of 2015 were with corporate companies or consultancy firms. Only 18 per cent were with NGOs.[28] In the US, of the 100 organisations that spend the most on lobbying annually, 90 per cent or more represent business interests. Many of the other non-business organisations claiming to speak for citizens lack much representation at all.[29]

When only large corporations or dominant non-business organisations can play the game, what chance do we have of influencing policy or politics? Challenging any existing policy that benefits or supports big business is increasingly difficult. So, if you want to change things, you'd better have powerful allies. However, the scale and rapidity of the growth in lobbying has outpaced the traditional forces that are supposed to keep it in check to protect us from undue influence exercised by dominant interests. Those forces include 'general interest intermediaries' like political parties and the media, as well as traditional civil society organisations such as trade unions, churches and community groups that stand up for the various public interests of consumers and taxpayers. They have undergone a massive transformation. Political parties, at least those that survive, no longer act as intermediaries between people and power; they are either part of the state apparatus or political movements committed to fighting it. The media, driven by the struggle for readers and viewers, has emerged as the key builder of social consensus. Yet, as the majority of news is consumed via social media, what each of us chooses to read fosters a false sense that everyone agrees with us. As predicted more than a decade ago by Cass Sunstein, our digital social existence has turned into a echo chamber, where we discuss similar views with like-minded peers and fail to penetrate other social bubbles that are often misled by fear and xenophobia.[30] This amplification of our respective views robs us of a truly democratic conversation. More critically, it empowers a new generation of 'polarisation entrepreneurs' ready to exploit confirmation biases.

As a result of the progressive disappearance of disintermediation bodies – which act as intermediaries between governments and citizens, such as political parties, trade unions and media – civil society has lost ground. Civil society organisations spend a tiny fraction of their budgets on advocacy and, in any event, cannot afford to lobby at the same

level as corporate players. The subsequent gap in civic empowerment is disturbing. Political power is distributed in vastly
unequal ways. A US report on inequality noted that: 'Citizens
with low or moderate incomes speak with a whisper that is
lost on the ears of inattentive government, while the advan-
taged roar with the clarity and consistency that policymakers
readily heed'.[31]

The effects of this gap explain why so many of us feel
estranged from public life:

1. Under a democratic model exclusively sustained and
   driven by elections, *citizens are encouraged to remain
   passive.* They merely respond to a cacophony of signals.
   While liberal democracies still hold elections regularly, the debate and overall public discourse is a tightly
   controlled performance, managed by professional communication advisors, and increasingly dependent on
   data-driven political marketing via social media.[32] The
   result is what British sociologist Colin Crouch described
   as 'post-democracy'.[33]

2. Due to the growing weight of the lobbying game, *citizens have lost their prerogative when it comes to collective
   governance.* In the absence of a space for citizens or motivation to act, they are no longer in a position to bring
   about social change through the traditional channels of
   participation. As the economist William Nordhaus has
   noted, there is 'no mechanism by which global citizens
   can make binding collective decisions'.[34]

3. *Policies are condemned to failure if the people at the receiving end do not inform them.* Cutting off the governing elites from popular influence lets their members exercise expertise, experience and wisdom independently. But it leads to poor decisions. How can policymakers solve a problem without hearing the voice of those who are the most affected by it? And how do they know whether it is a problem in the first place? The culture of real-time reporting, spurred by social media, does not necessarily make the lives of policymakers – especially of elected representatives – any easier. While social media gives citizens a voice, their input – because it is not mediated through the policy process – often becomes an indecipherable cacophony.

4. Because they are deaf to the general public (preferring the affluent, the organised or the most vocal), *policymakers are often ideologically biased and driven by short-term interests.* Winning the next election is more important than delivering on the promises made in the last. Responding to a sudden spark of protest against a policy proposal is more important than pointing out its underlying merits. Given the dramatic gap between the dominant quick-fix culture and our needs as a society, this is all the more troubling.

5. *Public policies lack legitimacy,* insulated as they are from the public's influence. Due to the opacity characterising decision-making procedures, only a select few can claim

ownership of a new piece of legislation or initiative. And usually those who feel this ownership are those who don't acknowledge it, but who in fact had a decisive influence – often by drafting texts for the policymakers.

Put simply, the decisions our representatives take are often not in the public interest. They are shaped by those who can afford to shout the loudest and represent only a handful of partisan interests, many of which run counter to the public good. This is coupled with the fact that citizens have become more and more cut off from the institutions that are supposed to represent them.

As a result, we are witnessing a crisis of political representation throughout the world. Low turnout, electoral volatility and crisis-ridden political parties are some of the more obvious symptoms of this disease. We have not only grown more critical of our political leaders but have also become more cynical about the value of democracy as a political system and have thus become less hopeful that anything we do might influence public policy.[35] The graph on the next page portrays the percentage of people rating it essential to live in a country that is governed democratically, by age cohort (decade of birth).

Young people are especially disengaged. According to the International Institute for Democracy and Electoral Assistance (IDEA), global voter turnout is lowest among 18–29 year-olds – a trend observable not only in developed democracies, but also in emerging ones.[36] At an IDEA forum hosted in 1999, 100 young people were asked their opinion

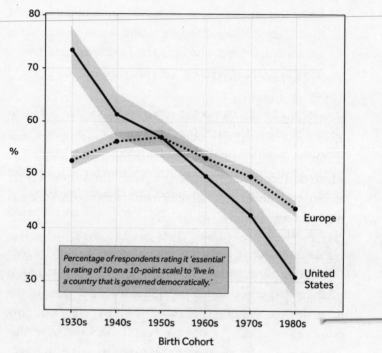

Percentage of respondents rating it 'essential' (a rating of 10 on a 10-point scale) to 'live in a country that is governed democratically.'

Source: World Values Surveys, Waves 5 and 6 (2005–14)

on youth participation in politics. Their answers revealed the extent of their disengagement:

Participants noted several factors affecting youth participation in politics, from not understanding how the system works, to a growing distrust of political institutions and leaders, to a lack of time in today's competitive environment. They also emphasized that they are not apathetic about politics but rather that they feel alienated from traditional political processes and are not convinced their participation can make a difference.

Most of us have indeed lost interest in public life and our ability to contribute to it – even though we could if we chose to do so. And even though we know that a more egalitarian political process would result in a more egalitarian society. The interest group theory theorised and advocated by James Madison,[37] Alexis de Tocqueville[38] and Robert Dahl[39] shows how a fairer society gives under-represented groups more power. So, making civic engagement more equal must be a crucial part of any solution to this disengagement. We should never be reduced to believing that only a comfortable elite can influence policy and politics. Part II of the book will provide more detail on how to revamp civic engagement to contribute to a fairer society.

You're Not in the Club: the Gap Between You and Your Representatives

'I've always tried to explain democracy is not perfect.
But it gives you a chance to shape your own destiny.'
Aung San Suu Kyi

Who are the people who claim to represent us?

Most of them are white males, and their lives and backgrounds are far removed from the world most of us inhabit. Ordinary life is an unknown entity to most of our elected representatives. Across the world, more and more people are going into politics straight from university. The non-career politician is an endangered species. This leads to a loss of experience, moderation and judgement, as we are increasingly governed by people with a diminished experience of the world beyond politics. The vast majority never have to face the threat of unemployment, street violence or the struggle to pay the bills. This is not to suggest that politicians don't care about us. But the truth is that by the time they make it to public office, they have largely forgotten what it's like to be an ordinary citizen.

Much of the distance between voter and elected official stems from the fact that representative democracy has come of age. As we have seen, behind the original idea of representation was the legitimate belief that only a well-trained elite group of individuals, insulated from citizens' emotional responses, and having gained knowledge from studying and traveling the world, were capable of making the best decisions for the rest of society. While this system – often referred to as a 'technocracy' – might have had some logic in the past (and did indeed work for some time), in today's society, where knowledge is largely shared and can be acquired in just a few clicks, it is outdated. Instead, by distancing actual decision-making from everyday people and delegating it to an elite group, our democratic system has helped foster disconnect between the voters – who became laymen – and the elected – who became professional politicians. As knowledge becomes steadily more democratised, very few citizens really believe that our elected representatives are experts who alone possess the wisdom and skills needed to solve problems. Not even the most charismatic leaders succeed in holding the respect of the public for any considerable length of time.

Yet a few figures have recently managed to energise young people and engage them in democracy by taking an overtly 'anti-establishment' stance. Bernie Sanders in the US and Jeremy Corbyn in the UK have both galvanised young people. They are not the only ones. Four other unconventional politicians have spearheaded youth movements precisely because they reject the mould of the traditional politician.

Jón Gnarr, Iceland

In the wake of the financial crisis of 2008, Jón Gnarr founded The Best Party as a jokey backlash against the ruling elite in Iceland. Initially intended as political satire, the party went on to win a majority on the Reykjavik City Council in 2010 and developed into Bright Future, which now holds six seats in Iceland's national parliament.

Tiririca, Brazil

With a nickname meaning 'Grumpy' and slogans like 'it can't get any worse', Tiririca won a seat in the Brazilian Congress as a federal deputy for São Paolo on an anti-elite ticket in 2010. Raised in a very poor family in the north of the country, Tiririca was a circus clown and TV comedian before entering politics. During the election campaign, he asked voters: 'What does a federal deputy do? Truly, I don't know. But vote for me and I will find out for you.'

Mhairi Black, UK

Mhairi Black was twenty years old when she won a seat in the 2015 UK general election. The average age of a British MP is

50, making Black by far one of the youngest ever, and she was elected with a massive 27 per cent swing from the incumbent. Young, lesbian and state-educated, she certainly doesn't fit the mould of the old, male, privately-educated politician that she and her Scottish National Party reject.

Erin Schrode, USA

Having co-founded an environmental non-profit at the age of thirteen, Erin also led education projects and peace-building movements early on. As a firm believer in representative (!) democracy, Erin was frustrated by the fact that 51 per cent of the US population are women and 35 per cent are under the age of 30, yet there had never been a woman under 30 elected to the United States Congress. In 2016, Erin launched a congressional campaign as a 24-year-old woman and was the youngest person ever to do so in the US. Although she lost the primaries in California, Erin gained international attention from media and politicians and forced her competitors to address the youth-relevant issues of her agenda. Erin is preparing to run in the next election cycle.

And yet many of our elected representatives regard themselves as belonging to a different class. They live and act outside the common life. They derive their authority from elections and proximity to influential circles rather than from erudition and learning. Their alleged superiority is based on the fact they belong to a governing elite made up of corporate leaders, journalists and other influential actors who court their favours. They all go to the same parties, read the same books, send their kids to the same schools and rarely take public transport. As this circle of the happy few draws closer and closer, their distance from the rest of the world grows exponentially.

Psychology offers some insights into why this distance exists, in particular, illustrating why politicians are increasingly unable to understand the ordinary citizen's experience. Alarmingly, these mechanisms apply to all of us, regardless of our best intentions.[40]

According to social identity theory, our attitudes and behaviour in life are determined by our sense of identification with a group (the 'in-group'). Because they perceive themselves as part of the governing class, politicians not only take a benign view of their colleagues, but look on everyone else – 'the out-group', i.e. citizens – less positively. As a result, the people in power become less and less capable of empathy. Since, by definition, problem-solving requires a thorough understanding of the people affected by an issue, this is very problematic.

How can we possibly expect politicians to solve our problems when they are not *their* problems? How can they grasp the consequences of their decisions on our lives?

The condescending view they hold of the rest of us certainly doesn't encourage us to interact with our 'representatives', to share our problems, keep track of their actions (or inaction) or gain a better understanding of the challenges faced by society. The growing distance between them and us instead stokes deep-seated feelings of powerlessness, detachment and even anger towards our representatives, which is at the heart of the growing lack of interest in public life.

We are constantly reminded that we are 'not in the club'. We are the out-group. We are the spectators. We'll address how to counteract such a feeling of powerlessness in the next section of the book.

Nobody Teaches You (to Act like a Citizen)

> 'I hear and I forget. I see and I remember.
> I do and I understand.'
> Confucius

From the early days of Western civilisation, dating back to Plato and Aristotle, education has been regarded as essential to the training of good citizens and the cultivation of a proper attachment to the state. It is not just about study and reflection, but also uncovering individual talent and applying it for the benefit of the whole of society. Public education therefore should not only aim to teach an individual to succeed, but also to participate in community life.[41]

However, at school, hardly anybody prepares you for informed, engaged participation in public life. Most of the time, we don't have the chance to experience what it is like to participate in the political process, in our community or in wider society. True, some of you might have had a 'citizenship' lesson. Done well, civic education not only teaches the civic knowledge and skills we need to keep our democracy safe, but also builds the techniques most needed in the global knowledge economy – things like effective communication, collaboration and critical thinking.

Yet the evidence suggests that no country has managed to give its citizens enough understanding and awareness of their rights and responsibilities to adequately preserve democracy.

Democracy is not 'a machine that would go of itself'.[42] As Alexis de Tocqueville reminded us, each new generation is a 'new people' who must acquire the knowledge, learn the skills and develop the right private and public temperament to underpin any constitutional democracy.

Yet most schools focus on passing on knowledge in traditional subjects rather than on developing practical skills. Generally, schools do a good job at preparing technically competent people, but they promote a 'me-first' culture, training us to act as detached experts providing a service for people, not as citizens working with others to solve public problems. The dominant educational model reflects the values of the highly individualistic and achievement-oriented middle-class. It treats students as largely passive clients, not as creative agents who have the potential to solve actual problems. As a result, there is no connection between the classroom experience, the curriculum and community engagement. Much of our widespread feeling of powerlessness has its roots in this disjunction between what we teach and what we need to know to succeed as a modern society. In particular, we are witnessing a growing and well-documented gap between what schools, including universities, offer us and what today's society (and the workplace) expects from us.

We are taught to look at the world from the specific angle of our profession or discipline – engineering, plumbing, art, media, law, communication or economics.[43] But we tend to be embarrassingly illiterate when it comes to public life. As a result, not only do we lack the confidence and fluency to assert our power as citizens, but – worse – we are unaware this power even exists. We have to struggle to resist the seduction of a popular culture that expresses contempt for entering public life, dismissing it as political ambition or a shortcut to a 'proper job'. Schools in turn reinforce society's dominant belief that the only ways to play a role in public life are to vote and to run for office. By denying the existence of any space between these two forms of participation, the education system not only fails to fulfil its civic mission, but damages our civic foundations.

My experience both as a student and as a professor has left me with a discouraging impression of what education does for us. Students seem as jaded as the rest of us when it comes to the traditional business models of education and politics. However, faced with the familiar demands to listen, read, write and study, students are increasingly asking: 'Why?' Sometimes they even dare to ask: 'What for?' They are more and more aware that the school system can no longer artificially separate learning and society. They want to learn less from the teacher and more from hands-on, real-life experiences, to write more, and to be more actively involved in their education – possibly by co-authoring their curriculum and tailoring it to the needs of society.

Schools can no longer afford to teach theories without showing how to apply them. The time has come to teach non-cognitive, social and emotional skills, such as self-awareness (the ability to recognise one's emotions),

self-management (the ability to control them), social awareness (the ability to empathise with people from diverse
backgrounds and cultures) and relationship skills (the ability to maintain healthy and rewarding relationships with
them).[44]

It's not all one-sided. The academic community more
broadly wants to connect with their communities, be exposed
to the culturally rich, pluralistic and ethnically diverse world
we live in, and do so regardless of class or income. They want
to ensure that their work doesn't just advance academic debate
but has an impact on the real world. Demand for 'impact' is
growing across the sciences and 'impact teaching',[45] as well as
policy-driven work, sounds more attractive than it used to.

But let's be frank. Education and research driven by impact
and policy attract more suspicion than praise in today's academic community. Scholars who embrace this approach risk
jeopardising their reputation for rigorous scholarship. There
is an assumption that proximity to and direct engagement
with the object of study would impoverish rather than enrich
the scientific value of their work. The word 'activism' is often
used pejoratively.

As both a teacher and a scholar, I find it difficult to accept
this position. I will never forget walking into my European
Affairs classroom at 8am on 24 June 2016, the day after the
UK voted to leave the European Union. It was one of the most
thought-provoking classes I ever experienced. By linking
theory to action, we spent hours speculating about the immediate effects of the vote on my students' lives and the world.
There is nothing more enriching than sharing a research topic

with a classroom of future problem-solvers. I see it in the students' eyes. They love it when the real world comes into the classroom and calls on them for solutions. And evidence backs them up: the more you are involved in the learning experience, the more you learn.

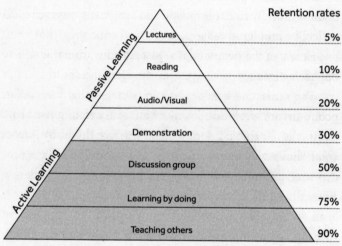

Source: Alberto Alemanno, adapted from figures from the World Bank, and from National Training Laboratories, Bethel, Maine.

But learning is not just about retention rates. Studies suggest that students do far better in academic and social terms when they are exposed to settings which encourage influences from outside the academy.[46] In particular, participation in extra-curricular activities has a positive correlation with students' attendance, grade point average test scores and expected educational goals.[47] Researchers at California State University, Sacramento, proved this to be true both at a high school and university level.[48] This is why I have emphasised experiential learning in my teaching – learning through reflection on action.

In sum, we should not just measure the return on our investment in education in terms of individual success, but on how much the next generation of citizens is prepared to fix collective problems collaboratively and creatively.

How can we persuade a reluctant educational world to engage with this urgent need for civic participation?

The same skills most needed in the global knowledge economy are the ones we need to preserve our civic and democratic life. It is exactly by embracing this shift – from *what you know* to *what you can do* – that we can overcome our widespread feeling of powerlessness and lack of control. But we need more than a paradigm shift.

Education can do much more for society than it does today. Students must be taught to act *with* citizens (by listening and working with them), and not *upon* them (by fixing their problems, arbitrating their disputes, building their homes, convincing them to consume), so they can engage with the civic life of their communities. The talents and intelligence of people who we've previously judged to lack the 'right' qualifications must be recognised. Professionals' citizenship must be cultivated, not weakened. We must all learn to see our work in communal and public terms.

By reconnecting with the real world, education can empower each of us, not as spectators but as world actors.

Somebody Decides for You: Powerless by Design

'What is freedom? Freedom is the right to choose:
the right to create for oneself the alternatives
of choice. Without the possibility of choice
and the exercise of choice, a man is not a man
but a member, an instrument, a thing.'
Archibald MacLeish

Life is about choices: what to eat, what to read, who to vote
for, what to buy, where to live. Our innate ability to choose is
fundamental to our sense of ourselves as human beings. We
like to think we live in freedom-loving societies. We like having choices because it makes us feel in control and therefore
powerful – even though we now know that too much choice
makes people unhappy.[49]

Although we cannot always choose in life, when we do so
we generally consider ourselves good at it. We tend to pause
and ponder the costs and benefits of different options before
making up our minds. Yet our ability to make rational choices
is increasingly being questioned, as we discover more about
cognitive biases – the predictable mechanisms that prevent
us from acting in our own best interests. In our busy lives,
these mechanisms work as 'mental shortcuts' by easing the
cognitive load of making a decision.[50] They were originally
identified by Daniel Kahneman and Amos Tversky in a sem-
inal article published in the magazine *Science* in 1974. This
led Kahneman, after the premature death of Tversky, to win
the Nobel Prize for Economics in 2002.[51]

Let me share a few examples of the major cognitive biases

that affect our daily behaviour. As a teacher, I regularly see my students taking these mental shortcuts. So if I ask: 'How many members of the European Union have adopted the Euro currency? More or less than ten?', my students will use the figure of ten countries as a reference point in coming to a conclusion. Behavioural scientists call the numerical figure that people use to make decisions an anchor. As the right response is nineteen,[52] my hint is potentially misleading, as students infer the number to be somewhere between five and fifteen. When I don't prompt them with the figure of ten, the range of responses is typically broader (between six and 28 states).

Here's another example. You go to the doctor for a check-up. He tells you that you need surgery. Before agreeing, you immediately ask about the likelihood of the operation being successful. The doctor knows the answer, and he can convey it to you in either of these ways: (a) 90 per cent of patients are fine, or (b) 10 per cent face complications. If he uses (a), 70 per cent of patients will accept the intervention, but if he chooses (b) only 35 per cent will.

What this illustrates is the framing effect – how the way choices are presented influences our decisions in life. In other words, context matters. This applies whether you're picking a mortgage, going shopping, posting on social media or going to the polls. Rearranging a food display can make you more likely to choose the healthy option. Publishing an image next to your Facebook or Twitter posts makes them more likely to be read and liked.

Have you begun to doubt your ability to be in full control of your choices?

How free *are* we when we choose? And is it really us who is doing the choosing?

Mental shortcuts can be even sneakier. Inertia means we tend to stick to default settings and rules. When you download a new operating system and are prompted to choose the recommended version, you go with the suggestion. Of course, you *can* opt out and manually download a different OS instead, but very few people will. Likewise, if you are offered the chance to renew a mobile phone plan, it is very unlikely that you will change it, even when it would be in your best interest and it could be done fairly easily. Small hurdles matter a lot.

One consequence is that people have a strong tendency to stick to the default option. In some cases this default option is set by law, but most of the time it is left to the market. The best example is organ donation. Where the law presumes consent and people have to opt out of the scheme (explicitly refuse to donate their organs), the proportion of donors in the population is much higher than where people have to opt in (sign up to a register as a donor).[53] As a result, many countries are switching from opt-in systems to opt-out systems. The same thing is happening for things like magazine subscription renewals and pension schemes. The default situation matters.

Social influence (or peer pressure) is another important factor. Our natural tendency to adjust to the dominant behaviour of a group – often called 'herd behaviour' – explains why you often act differently when in company. Social context matters too. So if the framing effect explains why we pick food that is closer and easier to see, social influence makes us eat more of it when we are with other people.[54]

These mental shortcuts – anchoring, framing, the power of inertia, defaults as well as social influence – are often called heuristics. Because of our cognitive laziness, we constantly (and unconsciously) rely on these mental shortcuts when making decisions, including, of course, decisions about our political leaders and civic life. Which is why it's worth getting to know a few more heuristics, so you can become aware of their influence on your behaviour.

Among the most common cognitive biases, one could mention:

a. *Availability heuristic*: events that come to people's mind immediately are rated as more probable (i.e. a recent plane crash) than events that are less mentally available.

b. *Probability neglect*: the tendency to completely disregard probability when making a decision under uncertainty (for example, in the year following 9/11, 1,595 Americans died in car accidents, as they were more inclined to drive than fly).

c. *Confirmation bias*: the tendency to search for or interpret information in a way that confirms one's preconceptions or hypothesis. As a result, this leads to overconfidence in personal beliefs and can maintain or strengthen beliefs in the face of contrary evidence.

d. *Loss aversion*: people's inherent propensity to strongly prefer avoiding losses to making gains. Thus, in experiments, most subjects would prefer to receive a sure $46 than have a 50 per cent chance of making $100. A rational agent would take the bet. Would you?

e. *The sunk-cost fallacy*: people seek to avoid feelings of regret; thus, they invest more money and time in a project with dubious results rather than give it up and admit they were wrong.

f. *Status quo bias*: the tendency to like things to stay relatively the same.

g. *Optimism bias*: the tendency to be over-optimistic, overestimating your ability to commit and deliver so as to attain favourable outcomes (I am definitely a victim!).

h. *Omission bias*: the tendency to judge harmful actions as worse, or less moral, than equally harmful omissions (inactions).[55]

Like Homer Simpson, we think much less than we think we think. The more we know about these findings, the more powerless we are likely to feel. As one of the leading researchers in the field, Daniel Ariely, explains:

> Behavioural economics is depressing because it shows us that we are just not that wonderful. It shows us that we are myopic, vindictive, that we don't know what we want, that we are easily confused, it shows all the mistakes we can make.[56]

This can be an unsettling discovery. Realising the power that doctors have over patients or the ability of town planners to influence the number of road accidents is arresting. Behavioural science can be used for good or bad. While it can ensure more people receive organ transplants, it can also be used to make you carry on subscribing to a magazine even though you no longer read it, or make you click on a Google AdWord. (That's the ubiquitous ad that appears when you do a search on Google.)

It won't surprise you to learn that marketers have been exploiting mental shortcuts for some time. They do so by steering our choices towards their best financial interests.[57] If you have ever watched the US TV series *Mad Men* (you should!), you will recognise this. Marketers routinely make us engage in actions we would never willingly have taken without their prompting. Sometimes they trick us into buying items we don't need, or into choosing more expensive options. In short, they help us choose what they want us to buy. The same tricks are used to steer political behaviour. The merging of politics and consumer marketing has been happening for half a century, originally through direct mail campaigns aimed at personalising political messages.

While companies and politicians have been exploiting our mental shortcuts for quite some time, the ability of marketers to take decisions on your behalf has grown exponentially. While mental shortcuts don't explain everything we do, our habits, routines and social interactions are surprisingly predictable, not least because marketers collect thousands of pieces of metadata about each of us, including our purchase data and online browsing habits. By playing with this data, it is possible to actually predict future consumer – and increasingly political – behaviour. As a result, our behaviour and choices are increasingly steered by micro-targeting. This consists of personalised advertisements and search results and e-commerce recommendation systems like Amazon's. You might have heard the story of how a supermarket, Target, worked out a teenage girl was pregnant before her father did.[58] Target's consumer tracking system identified 25 products that when purchased together indicate a woman is likely to be expecting a baby. The value of this information was that Target could send coupons to the pregnant woman at an expensive and habit-forming period of her life. That is targeted marketing.

Society's ability to collect, process and analyse information in new ways to generate valuable insights is generally referred to as big data.[59] As a result of the commodification of big data, companies can increasingly manipulate our decisions, behaviour and feelings.[60] And they are already doing so.

This emerging phenomenon is not driven exclusively by economic motives. Critically, it is not confined to the market. Governments increasingly embrace big data – triangulating the openly shared personal information from about a dozen social media sites – in order to inform the police, or shut down protests in real time.

We know that Facebook conducted experiments to encourage people to vote in US elections from at least 2010 onwards. By prompting users to publish 'I voted' updates, the social network was nudging Americans to carry out their civic duty. The underlying mechanism of the 'voter megaphone' was social influence and peer pressure to vote. In so doing, researchers tapped into tens of millions of pieces of data to identify the most effective ways of encouraging voting. It turned out that, largely due to social influence and herd behaviour, notifications from friends were what most influenced people's behaviour. After comparing voting records, the experiment is estimated to have led to 340,000 extra voters.[61] Needless to say, this is more than the extra votes a candidate usually needs to win a swing state in the US.

The intentions may be good. The hope is that big data can improve our lives and revamp governance by overcoming irrationality and biased debates. Yet systematic reliance on it evokes philosopher Immanuel Kant's warning: the 'sovereign acting ... to make the people happy according to his notions ... becomes a despot'.[62] It is for this reason that the US Declaration of Independence emphasises individuals' pursuit of happiness, while EU foundational treaties aim to improve their wellbeing – a marker that can be more objectively assessed.

Facebook primarily collects all this information in order to tailor ads to sell us stuff we want – and then sells them to advertisers, simply because the company can make a lot of money doing so. But the influence of data-driven architectures of choice extends beyond our individual and market behaviour. It may even affect our deeper emotional states.

In 2012, Facebook manipulated the news feeds of nearly 700,000 people to see if the emotions prompted by the content affected the emotion they then displayed through their own posts.[63] To run the week-long experiment, some Facebook users were exposed to less positive emotional content on their news feed than usual. Others saw less negative emotional content. Facebook then tracked users' posts after they were exposed to the manipulated news feeds. Although legal (when you sign up for Facebook, you authorise it to use your data for analysis and research), many people found the experiment unethical, because they were unaware of it.

For those of you who still believe that the posts you see on your Facebook feed (or in the results of your Google search) are listed in chronological order, this story might come as a genuine surprise. You're in good company: the majority of users continue to believe that Facebook, Google and other major platforms are neutral go-betweens. They're not. Think for a moment of Google's autocomplete searches (when you type Alberto Alemanno, Google automatically suggests 'actor' so as to frame that search – needless to say, that's not me!), Netflix recommendations, Twitter Trends or OKCupid matches.

What these platforms offer is the product of an accurately engineered algorithm. This is a mathematically-powered application that optimises the outcomes chosen by its pro-grammers. After processing a bunch of data, an algorithm identifies patterns among the various data points it owns about you and then determines the probability that, for instance, you will pay back your mortgage, become an excellent employee or are interested in buying that car, song or book. In the case of Facebook – specifically its Newsfeed – the goal is to max-imise the amount of engagement you have with the site, and hence with advertisers. You are therefore selectively exposed to the posts you have the greatest propensity to 'like'. Every click generates revenue. This is the pay-per-click internet advertising model that defines your internet 'user experience'. You can find it on all the major platforms, including Google.

Algorithms need data just as cars need fuel. There are thousands of bodies that collect and sell personal information from website cookies, loyalty card programmes, pharmacy records and some of the 10 million public data and registries sets available. While each individual data point carries little meaning and value by itself, taken together they may enable the brokers to draw some powerful conclusions about you, and to create a profile which they sell to businesses who want to target their product or political advertisements. Facebook, for instance, acts both as a data buyer and data broker.

Algorithms are anything but objective. Being the products of human imagination, they embed a series of assumptions about how the world works and how it ought to work. They approximate the world in a way that suits the purposes of their architect. Thus, for instance, they typically rely on your credit score as a proxy to determine whether you will be a good employee. Similarly, a programmer may decide that people who read the *Guardian* are feminine and people who read tech blogs are masculine. These algorithms are unscientific, based on assumptions, but they increasingly shape your life.

As such, algorithms do not just encode biases, but per-petuate them. By relying on historical data, such as the fact that women and people from ethnic minorities earn less, they reflect and magnify those biases in society. For example, in Washington DC, wait times for Uber cabs are, in gen-eral, shorter in the centre of the District and longer in the periphery where more non-whites live.[64] This is due to Uber's surge-pricing algorithm which influences car availability by dynamically adjusting prices. When surge is in effect, and prices are higher, the idea is that the supply of drivers is increased while at the same time demand is decreased. Rather than increase the *absolute* supply of drivers by getting more cars on the road, existing driver supply is instead redistributed geographically to places with more demand. If drivers are relocating to areas with surge-pricing, those areas will experience reduced wait times for cars (better service), whereas the areas the drivers are moving away from will experience longer wait times (poorer service). So who gains, and who loses? Which neighbourhoods get consistently better or worse service? As a result of the algorithm, people living in predominantly non-white areas of the US have to wait longer for Uber cabs.[65]

Given how pervasive these mechanisms have become in our lives, and their potential to turn our lives upside down, you might expect to be able to appeal their decisions. But there is no way to challenge their results or even question their operation. Unfortunately, algorithms are black boxes, with their workings invisible to almost everyone except their programmers.[66] This opacity is made possible by a complex web of proprietary rights; for instance, Google algorithms are a secret as closely-guarded as the Coca-Cola recipe. We don't know the data that goes into them, how that data is processed through the algorithm, or the outcome – the value that emerges, be it a score, price or prediction. In short, algorithms remain largely untested, unquestioned and unregulated, which, troublingly, prevents users from contesting the quality of their underlying data, how it is obtained and the results.

Algorithms render us powerless by design. Every one of our actions (or omissions) is characterised by an asymmetry of information between *us* (constantly monitored) and the Silicon Valley titan of the moment (which monitors us).

What's more, machine learning is spreading rapidly. This technique enables computers to independently 'learn to learn' by guzzling massive amounts of rough data, including data we generate in digital environments.

Facial recognition software has even developed ways of reading our moods through our expressions and body language.[67] Tesco has already deployed technology capable of advertising different products to different customers, depending on how cameras capture their moods.[68] People walking past billboards can now see and hear real-time, personalised marketing which 'fits' their age and gender. As I learnt while teaching at Tokyo University, facial recognition is also used in the classroom to identify whether a student is bored or attentive.[69]

It gets worse. What happens when algorithms factor in our mental shortcuts so as to target a particular subset of the population? Take the phenomenon of fake news, which began as a consequence of the pay-for-clicks model. There is mounting evidence that these fabricated stories, which are designed to fool readers into sharing them so they go viral, are typically served to 'low-information voters'.[70] These are people who either know little about politics or lack what psychologists call a 'need for cognition'. In other words, they tend to make decisions based on mental shortcuts, such as 'experts' or other opinion leaders, rather than by thinking through an issue methodically. Companies like Cambridge Analytica build accurate psychological profiles of each of us, then create a political message tailored to our personalities.[71] In order to do this, the company doesn't need to interact directly with each of us; instead, it acquires information from data brokers (demographics, social media and consumer and lifestyle data) and runs models calibrated against other individuals who have completed psychological tests (Facebook runs these constantly). In so doing, Cambridge Analytica combines our online personas with our offline selves, a process that has now become so commonplace as to have acquired the name 'onboarding.'

That's a snapshot of the engine behind the opaque business of online micro-targeted propaganda. Even in long-established democracies like Italy, Germany and Spain, fake news reports and hate speech on social media have been used to feed grassroots populist movements.

These examples of the ubiquitous targeting to which we are now subjected nurture our feeling of powerlessness. When citizens feel battered by forces over which they have no control, they find it harder to achieve contentment in their lives. Increasingly little is left to chance in our surroundings – whether we are walking around a supermarket, or online. And this kind of surveillance is not confined to the marketplace. Governments use it too, as the Snowden leaks showed.

This is even more problematic for the weaker members of our societies. As lucidly shown by Eldar Shafir and Sendhil Mullainathan in *Scarcity*, those who struggle for insufficient resources – time, money, food, companionship – are typically the citizens worst affected by the exploitation of our cognitive limitations, and are therefore the major victims of targeting techniques.[72] Their mental capacity – Shafir and Mullainathan call it 'bandwidth' – is shrunk, taxed and left unable to cope with the onslaught. Being poor, they show, reduces your cognitive ability more than going a full night without sleep.

Injustices have always existed. But the ability to control individuals through the use of technology risks deepening our unprecedented social inequalities. Based on a combination of preferences, habits, postcodes and status updates, predatory algorithms enable marketers to target people in great need in order to identify where they suffer the most – what is called the 'pain point' – and to sell them false or overpriced promises. For years, online retailers like Amazon and travel companies like Expedia have priced items according to who they think we are, where we live, our incomes and our previous purchases. Often, paradoxically, the rich pay less. Yet there are signs that the rich as well as the poor are being targeted – because the low-information voters targeted by fake news, for example, exist at the top as well as the bottom of the income scale.

If you felt powerless when you picked up this book, I suspect you are now feeling even more adrift. While this may sound discouraging, this first part of the book is intended to make you react, to jolt you out of complacency. In the next sections we will show you how much power you have (Part II) and how unbelievably easy it is to exercise that power (Part III).

PART II

THE SOLUTION

The Power of
Citizen Lobbying

'I act on the conviction that everyone is
making a difference. Just by living our
lives, consuming space and resources,
we are making a difference. Our choice
is what kind of difference to make.'

Fran Peavey[1]

Now that we know *why* we increasingly feel so helpless
and powerless, it is time to look at *what* we can do about
it. How can we – as individuals and a society – stop being
spectators in our private and public lives? How can we secure
a place at the table, and more importantly ensure that everyone gets a place?

In order to find a solution, we need to explore the following questions: How do we make government work for us?
How can we save us from ourselves?

We face a dramatic gap between the problem-solving ability of our political system and our needs as a society. While
this gap explains much of our social disengagement and disillusionment with traditional politics, it opens up a promising
space for new, unconventional forms of active citizenship
and civic engagement, as well as individual and collective
empowerment.

This is the space we want and can occupy, as citizens. And it is set to grow as people abandon mainstream politics. That's the space I want to you show you in the second part of this book.

Given the inability of the current political system to represent you properly, the only option left is to speak out. To borrow Albert Hirschman's expression,[2] this is a time to 'voice', not to exit.

There has never been a better time and we have never been in a better place to speak out. We are more educated, well connected, purposeful and less deferential to authority than ever before. Regardless of where you come from and what you do in life, each of us has talents, expertise and experience that can be harnessed to the benefit of society.

And millennials care about social impact more than any previous generation[3]. The conventional political narrative – voting or running for office – has exhausted its authority. We need to come up with an innovative form of participation that enables someone like you and me – a student, a jobseeker, a professional or a pensioner – to speak out and channel her preferences into the existing policy process. And she needs to be able to do this part-time.

It might seem counter-intuitive, but if you want this kind of influence, you must turn yourself into a lobbyist. A citizen lobbyist. So what is lobbying about? How does it work? Can it really address our need to speak up for ourselves? And, finally, why would it work?

What is Lobbying and Who Does It?

'Eighty per cent of success is showing up.'
Woody Allen

Lobbying means persuading people who hold power to care
about an issue. Specifically, lobbying – more elegantly referred
to as advocacy – is the act of attempting to influence the
decisions made by policymakers, at any level of government.
A lobbyist can be anybody who seeks to influence policymakers in a given direction: she can work for a company,
represent the interests of a given industry or speak on behalf
of a non-governmental organisation (NGO). She might be
an employee of a lobbying firm, a lawyer acting for a client, a
policy analyst at a think-tank, a civic entrepreneur, a public
affairs consultant, or even an academic. Decision-makers can
be elected officials or civil servants, acting at a local, national
or even international level.

Lobbying is one of the most effective yet least-explored
ways to shape and influence (public) life. As such, it is likely
to have existed as long as politics itself – or at least as long as
the representative democracies many of us live in today. Some
say it is the second-oldest job in the history of humanity, after
prostitution. As soon as there are people who have the power
to make decisions on behalf of the whole community, there
will be somebody interested in influencing them.

Think about it. It is not enough to come up with a great
idea. You also need to sell it and galvanise support for it
through effective advocacy. This is as true in the business

world as it is in the business of government. The fate of many good and bad ideas that have shaped the world over the last century has largely been determined by lobbying. Consider how many good ideas, such as investment in lifesaving drugs for rare diseases, never became a reality because of poor advocacy. Think of how many bad ideas, like nuclear weapons, took off because of their successful advocacy. Contrary to Victor Hugo's famous line, 'an idea whose time has come' *can* be stopped. Depending on how it is used, lobbying can work for both good and bad.

Lobbying is something corporations excel at doing, and sometimes NGOs too. Citizens just don't do it. This explains why only a few people properly understand what lobbyists do and why.

The time has come to demystify this phenomenon. We need to free it from the widespread misinformation surrounding it, so it can be better understood and socially accepted.

STORY – Where Does the Word Lobby Come From?

The historical roots of the term 'lobby' date back to 1640 and refer to the place where British citizens could go to speak to their Member of Parliament (MP), the lobby of the House of Commons.

The United States has its own mythology around the genesis of lobbying. When President Grant was in office (1869–77), he used to visit the sumptuous lobby of the Willard Hotel in Washington DC to have a brandy and a cigar. Despite his best efforts to keep these trips private,

individuals in the hotel lobby would approach Grant
and ask him for special favours or jobs. President Grant
apparently referred to these people as 'lobbyists'.

While this story makes for an enjoyable anecdote,
the origin of the word 'lobbyist' cannot, in fact, be traced
to the lobby of the Willard Hotel. Rather, 'lobbyist' was
part of US vocabulary well before 1850, with the name
reportedly first used to refer to petitioners who would
wait to speak to legislators in the lobby of the New York
State Capitol in Albany. Furthermore, the word 'lobbying' can be found in print in the United States as far back
as 1820.

Lobbying has transformed itself into a multi-billion pound
industry and, as a result, we live in a lobbying-saturated (or
'lobbygenic') landscape.[4] We call it 'professional lobbying' to
distinguish it from other forms of lobbying, such as you pressuring your partner, friends or your elected representative.
Professional lobbying consists of paid professionals trying
to influence elected representatives to initiate – or block – a
given action, be it the decision to drill your area to obtain
gas, to secure a subsidy to support your industry or push for
someone to be appointed to high office. Lobbying is an omni-
present, powerful source of influence. As the billions invested
in it by multinationals suggests, lobbying has an impact on
all our lives.

In the US, around \$3.31 billion is spent each year on
lobbying. In the EU, Transparency International's conservative estimate puts it at around half that, or €1.5 billion.[5]

An Austrian Member of the European Parliament (MEP), Hans-Peter Martin, claims professional lobbyists spend as much as €10,000 per MEP per week on invitations and gifts for MEPs (there are 751 of them).[6]

Companies generally have their own 'in-house' lobbyists and also rely on lobbying advice from leading public affairs consultancies such as Burson & Marsteller, Holland & Knight and Ernst & Young.

Universities now offer courses in lobbying. I designed and have been teaching one since 2009 at my own university in Paris, the Ecole des Hautes Etudes Commerciales. Since 2014, I have also been offering a course at New York University that brings together a select group of law students from both NYU Law School and HEC Paris to work directly for NGOs operating in the EU policy field. The students are supported by a range of experienced and highly respected academics and practitioners who work with them on a pro bono basis to advance the goals of a select group of NGOs. Students are given the opportunity to play an active and important role in ongoing policy processes and advocacy campaigns concerning some of the most pressing issues facing the EU, its Member States and its 500 million inhabitants. In so doing, students help NGOs give voice to the often under-represented public interest in the complex supra-national EU policy process while finding personal gratification and meaning.

Every autumn I also offer a course devoted to lobbying at Tokyo University to a group of Masters students who have no legal background. As I teach my students, lobbying and its repertoire of tactics, techniques and practices is no longer the prerogative of major corporations. It belongs to anyone – including yourself – who is interested in influencing public authorities, and it is increasingly valued by a variety of players, including non-profit organisations, philanthropic foundations and social entrepreneurs. As a result of my advocacy evangelism, every year several of my students join NGOs, public affairs consultancies and public interest law firms. The latter, unlike commercial firms, pursue as their primary mission assisting under-represented people or causes, rather than making money.

Fundamentally, lobbying is a process by which advocates get together, formulate arguments, identify targets, select tactics and decide whether to work with others in an effort to bring about change. As we will see in Part III, there are techniques, tips and tricks that anyone can learn, but for now let's look at the basics of lobbying.

Think Tanks as Lobbyists

A think tank is essentially a university without students. It can carry out research and advocacy on a vast swathe of topics, ranging from social policy to political strategy, from economics to the military, technology and culture. Unsurprisingly, think tanks tend to be influential in policy debates. That's indeed their *raison d'être*.

Yet in the scramble for funds, think tanks often agree to push agendas important to their corporate donors, thereby blurring the line between objective research and goal-oriented lobbying. Think tanks sometimes agree to become vehicles for corporate (or less commonly, non-corporate) influence and branding campaigns on issues as various as international trade, real estate development and migration. If in the past donors did not attach conditions to their contributions, today they increasingly do.[7]

The problem is that when they agree to bend their research objectivity to accommodate vested interests, they reap the benefits of their tax-exempt or tax-favourable status, without necessarily disclosing their connections to corporate interests. It has become common practice for the conclusions of some think tank reports to be discussed with donors before their publication. Sometimes donors openly explain how the resulting 'scholarship' will be used as part of broader lobbying efforts.

Many think tanks in the EU receive a significant amount of funding from EU institutions for research projects whose intellectual independence is questionable.[8] On top of this public money, they also receive corporate sponsored contributions that make their work difficult to distinguish from lobbying.[9]

If the real value of a think tank should be to promote new and interesting ideas, think tanks' current proximity to corporate interests and their lack of transparency about it puts their ability to do so in question.

Despite this, their number and influence are growing. The United States – Washington DC in particular – boasts the largest pool of think tanks, and it has recently seen a proliferation of narrowly-focused outfits whose interests seem tied to specific industries. At the same time, the big names, such as

Brookings, the American Enterprise Institute and Cato, have experienced huge growth. While no other country has the same presence and variety of think tanks as the US, they are spreading across the world and increasingly play a lobbying role.[10]

In Europe, the number of think tanks has grown but, it is generally agreed, has not approached the critical mass and scientific quality of their transatlantic counterparts – apart from a few exceptions, notably in Brussels and the UK.[11] While US think tanks act as incubators for bright, promising newcomers with an outstanding academic record who are waiting to enter government for the first time, in the European space, many think tankers lack an academic profile and as a result are not perceived as completely independent.

Academics as Lobbyists

Through their writing, academics may also take a stance on a live policy issue and go on to influence its outcome. By leveraging their authority as credible and apparently independent authorities, they can effectively influence decision-makers. Unfortunately, as is the case with think tanks, the public is often unaware of the financial relationships between for-profit companies and the academics who testify before parliaments or speak at other public events. While it is common practice to disclose in a footnote of any scientific paper the origin of the funding that supported that research, this remains entirely voluntary.

Lobbying regulations in most countries largely ignore the phenomenon of academic lobbying. Yet there is mounting evidence about the existence of corporate-financed academic efforts, which are often aimed at sowing confusion and scepticism about scientific research.[12] Academics-turned-lobbyists are often called 'merchants of doubt', insofar as they are paid to twist the truth and inject doubt into the public debate. While this is not a new practice, today it can be found in all kinds of policy areas – ranging from e-cigarettes to the science of climate change.

Why Lobbying?

While we have already discussed the many problems with lobbying, there is a positive side to lobbying – especially when it comes to you finding your political voice. Indeed, while it must indisputably be regulated – by shedding light on *which* bodies lobby, *how*, at *whom*, and for *how much* – lobbying is a required component of any working democracy.[13]

How can lobbying, one of the culprits in our disillusionment with public life, actually empower you as a citizen? Three inter-related factors explain how. Each addresses a major shortcoming of the democratic system and makes a case for citizen lobbying.

1. Lobbying Works

When compared with actual representative democracy lobbying works because it enables anyone to directly voice her concerns. Lobbying is about persuading others, notably decision-makers, about the importance of that concern and to accept your solutions for how to address it. It means engaging actively with the policy process. It generally consists of putting pressure on elected representatives to initiate – or block – a certain policy, whether it is a decision to drill your area for gas, to launch reform of the pension system or to crack down on payday lenders. Through lobbying, you exercise two essential yet often neglected democratic functions: you communicate information while at the same time keeping tabs on your politicians. And it enables you to do so in between elections.

Moreover, unlike voting, where your preferences are all boiled down to a tick on the ballot sheet, lobbying lets you be specific about what you want, as well as letting you gather useful information. Because of its attention-grabbing nature, lobbying puts greater pressure on the representative to listen to you. As a result, she has much more reason to pay attention to you, the lobbyist, than to you, the voter.

While lobbying cannot guarantee that all voices will be listened to with equal attention, it can persuade elected representatives to change their priorities and take more people's interests into account, making the political game fairer.

James Madison, a Founding Father and the chief force behind the US Constitution, expressed this idea in *The Federalist Papers* in 1788. He suggested that lobbies (he called them factions) could be thwarted by requiring them to compete with other lobbies. He believed that the powerful force of one lobby could be counteracted by one or more others and that only as a result of this balancing exercise would good government emerge. From this perspective, the lobbying game can be understood as a check and balance on the workings of government. By preventing any group from having a permanent victory, it keeps a critical watch on power.[14]

2. Lobbying is for Everyone

Unlike actual electoral representative democracy, lobbying is something all of us can do. While only few individuals can run for elections (as they must usually sign up to a political party and enjoy a certain amount of wealth and influence), virtually everyone can try to persuade her representatives – or support a civil society organisation to do so. While professional lobbyists do tend to be qualified, there is nothing to stop you helping yourself from the lobbying toolbox. It does not require in-depth knowledge of how government works, but just a basic understanding of how to frame your cause to your elected representative. Anyone can tap into their personal interests, talents and network to push for a cause. At the heart of citizen lobbying is a deep belief in your own potential. Regardless of who you are, each of us can voice our concerns and channel them into the policy process.

Thanks to the information and digital revolution, lobbying is no longer the prerogative of well-funded groups with huge memberships and myriad political connections. In a famous 1997 judgement, the US Supreme Court emphasised the potential of the internet, arguing that 'through the use of chatrooms, any person with a phone line can become a town crier with a voice that resonates farther than it could from any soapbox'.[15] The internet's global reach is contributing to enormous advancements in democracy, social activism and advocacy.[16] As an individual, you can just as easily make an appointment with a politician to shape the policy process, denounce an injustice through an online campaign – and crowdfund it on the net – or inspire new forms of consumer and civic resistance on social media.

Many traditional channels of participation remain under-used by citizens – like public consultations and petitions – and further opportunities to participate in the policy process are growing all the time. It would be a pity not to seize the chance to ensure that they are not just tick-box exercises for our elected representatives, who can then claim they have listened to you.

Whether you are a young student or a senior professional, whether you work for an NGO or in the private sector, you've got more power than you may think. You may act alone or mobilise your community. You may also decide to team up with an existing organisation pursuing your cause, whether professional or amateur. In particular, by sharing your expertise with a pre-existing organisation, you can help people get their voices heard in government. NGOs are often under-resourced and understaffed, and might appreciate your help. This is particularly true given the multiplication of channels of influence – which call for more resources, expertise and time. Paradoxically, the creation of more opportunities to speak up and deliberate could end up favouring the usual suspects at the expense of the less-organised.[17]

3. Lobbying is Good for Society

> 'It is said that indirect lobbying by the pressure
> of public opinion on the Congress is an evil and
> a danger. That is not an evil; it is a good, the
> healthy essence of the democratic process.'
> Supreme Court decision in *Rumely v. United States, 1952*[18]

Contrary to conventional wisdom, lobbying is not only legitimate but is also necessary in a democracy. Transparency International, the leading anti-corruption organisation, expressly endorsed lobbying when it recognised in 2009 that:

> Lobbying provides useful information and opinions to political representatives and public officials. It is not, therefore, a morally questionable activity, but an important element of the democratic debate and decision-making process.

Despite the bad press it receives, lobbying is increasingly favoured today. This is part of a broader trend towards a more inclusive and participatory approach in the way governments work.

The main aim of the policy process is to ensure that the government pursues the public interest. But we can only find out what the public interest is with the help of those affected by regulation: citizens, businesses, consumers, NGOs, the public sector, international trading partners and others. Indeed, although citizens' involvement is a prerequisite for the good functioning of any democratic system, it is only recently that the value of open and inclusive policymaking has been widely accepted.[19] For too long, voting was regarded as the limit of public participation in policymaking and the policy process a top-down affair.

But today we are witnessing a new political moment in which citizen participation is no longer the assumed domain of outsiders but has become widely encouraged, if not directly mandated, by governments and international organisations. Now, more and more people think and expect they should play a more active role in government decision-making between elections.[20] Yet this happened – at least from the public authorities' perspective – more out of administrative necessity than idealism. The old ideal of an omniscient government, cognisant of its citizens' needs and capable of governing alone, is no longer tenable. It has become clear that making decisions without the public's backing can lead to confrontation, disputes, disruption, boycotts, distrust and public dissatisfaction.[21] As a result, the policy process has been opened up to virtually anyone who is willing to devote some of their time to comment and make observations. Those may be individual citizens or organised groups such as trade unions, consumer organisations and of course companies, and are collectively referred to as 'stakeholders'. Nowadays, we are all able – at least on paper – to lobby our public officials and governments.

Lobbying plays a crucial role at two different stages in the policy process: information gathering and rule-making. Firstly, it enables everyone potentially affected by a decision to provide information during the preparation phase. How can a policymaker know how a particular problem, such as the magnitude or frequency of natural disasters prompted by global warming, will unfold? How can she predict how a particular reform (e.g. limiting emissions) may affect the environment or the labour market (e.g. the number of people hired or sacked)? As such, lobbying acts as a corrective force that reinforces electoral-representative democracy. How can a policymaker take a decision about a new policy without having heard from those most affected by it? How can she ensure she has taken everyone's interests into account? Parties with a vested interest will probably give a better idea of its potential impact.

In this way, lobbying aims to guarantee that the policy process is well-informed, accountable and more inclusive.

But the benefits of engaging with all these stakeholders extend beyond the information-gathering phase. Failing to listen to the public in the rule-making process can lead regulators into difficulty, inefficiencies and lead them to overlook solutions they hadn't considered. Furthermore, public participation makes compliance more likely by building legitimacy into regulatory proposals. It can therefore make regulation more effective and cut the cost of enforcing it.[22] Lobbying can also lead to more creative and innovative policies, as stakeholders outside government – like you – are more likely to come up with non-traditional solutions. As management expert Adam Grant puts it, it is non-conformists who change the world.[23]

Yet a great deal of the promise and benefits of citizen engagement have yet to bear fruit. Public consultations are typically top-down exercises involving a few actors, often well-organised corporate interests, and which fail to engage the groups most affected by the policy at stake. Those are the people I call the 'missing stakeholders'.[24]

That is why we need not only to open up these participatory channels to the public, but also to make sure that everyone can actually gain access to them. Chris Welzel and Russell J. Dalton demonstrated that societies which enable citizens to be assertive and critical of public authorities tend to have governments that are more effective and accountable.[25] As they argue, governments are like waiters in a noisy restaurant: to get their attention you have to speak up. But to call a waiter you need first to gain a seat at the table!

Given how few people engage with their elected representatives, those who write a letter or send an email, monitor their pledges and check on their actions can have a disproportionate effect on what gets done and what is neglected. That means you have more power than you think. Regardless of how busy you are, you can learn how to actually use it in your daily life. The time has come to democratise lobbying by learning how to do it.

Let's see what being a citizen lobbyist involves, and how you could become one.

What is Citizen Lobbying?

> 'I'm tired of hearing it said that democracy doesn't work.
> Of course it doesn't work. We are supposed to work it.'
> Alexander Woollcott

As we've now seen, citizen lobbying is lobbying *by* citizens *for* citizens. In a nutshell, it involves you pushing for a cause or interest with your elected official, or through another participatory channel, to correct an unfair or harmful situation affecting the community. Thanks to the pressure you apply, the situation may be resolved through persuasion, compromise or through political or even legal action.

But what does citizen lobbying mean in practice? It is about you picking up the phone, sending an email or setting up a Twitter account (generally more effective) to reach decision-makers. It is about you filing a petition or creating a Facebook group to promote your cause. It is about you monitoring how a particular issue – whether the right of refugees not to be stripped of their possessions when they enter a new country, or the protection of birds – is handled by the political process. So it might involve you acting on your own for a cause you care deeply about, or you might represent another person's needs as if they were your own. But you might also provide support, by sharing your talent, expertise and some of your spare time, to an NGO like ActionAid, the WWF or a smaller NGO. It may entail getting other people involved – friends, neighbours, patients or victims of a particular problem – to voice their concerns.

Remember how student Max Schrems succeeded in challenging Facebook in Europe? He initially crowdfunded his project online. That enabled him to create a community of supporters around him and bring his challenge before the Irish authorities. Remember how my students and I managed to put on the agenda the elimination of roaming charges on mobile phones? A petition was lodged and the media attention did the rest.

Through citizen lobbying, anyone can acquire political clout and influence the democratic process. But unlike professional lobbying, citizen lobbying belongs to the broader, though ill-defined, phenomenon generally referred to as 'activism'. Indeed, like other forms of activism, it is unpaid and demands your time and commitment. And you give it out of belief.

Yet lobbying by the citizens differs from general activism in one important regard. Citizen lobbyists tap into the repertoire of techniques generally used by professional lobbyists to induce systemic change. Thus, while a sit-in protest expressing solidarity with the rejection of twelve new refugees in your city is activism, an online petition calling for a reform of the legal status of refugees is citizen lobbying.

In particular, what characterises citizen lobbying – as distinct from other forms of activism – are:

- the target (public authorities);
- the method (the lobbying toolkit); and
- the goal (systemic change).

Citizen lobbying chiefly targets public authorities, as they hold the key to systemic change. And to do this, it mobilises the toolbox of tactics and avenues of participation generally used by professional lobbyists. To clarify this second feature of citizen lobbying, if you join a group that helps build houses for the poor, it's great work. But it's not lobbying – it's a service. You're not targeting the policymakers, you're not using the lobbying toolbox and you're not changing the system – just fixing the problem for a few people. But if you instead start campaigning for a new housing policy for the poor by targeting the relevant policymakers, you are lobbying. While helping individual citizens to get a house is great and needed, it might be significantly more impactful if you fix a housing policy that will address the needs of virtually all homeless citizens.

Citizen lobbyists typically engage in the policy process by monitoring the policy process, identifying the issues of importance to them, developing a strategy and engaging in a variety of activities to attain their goal, often by mustering external support. Indeed, any effort aimed at monitoring and identifying a policy problem, shaping a solution and making it happen qualifies as citizen lobbying. The same is true when the efforts are directed at blocking, altering or boycotting a policy initiative. A citizen lobbyist does the same things as conventional lobbyists: monitoring, meeting with officials, strategic advocacy, coalition building, campaigning and more. The same thing happens when someone supports an existing group or NGO to pursue a cause by sharing their skills, expertise, time and energy. You become their lobbyist, while remaining a citizen.

Last but not least, what distinguishes a citizen lobbyist is her agnostic and pragmatic motivation. What drives her is not the desire to push an ideological agenda (e.g. being against free trade), but the desire to address an issue of public concern which has typically been neglected (e.g. how to ensure free trade benefits everyone).

A citizen lobbyist strives to advance the interests and

causes of the disadvantaged and as such it empowers everyone. This does not mean that citizen lobbing can realistically give all citizens an equal voice, but rather that all electors-elected relationships are going to be structured from that idea. Citizen lobbying nurtures commitment to a process in which a multiplicity of voices can be heard and all can help to set the 'rules of the game'.[26]

The genius of it is that it does this by channelling democratic distrust into a positive force. Unlike other traditional forms of activism, the concept of citizen lobbying reconciles protests and proposals. Participation begins not from a place of conflict but from one of shared interest. The elected representative listens to what others say and then decides what is best.

As a citizen lobbyist, you aim to set the agenda by prompting policymakers to act, but you can also react to the agenda set by government officials (or other forces). You put forward a solution to the problem identified. You may be confrontational (by resorting to pressure tactics and creative ways to get attention, when needed), cooperative and even deliberative.

To sum up, lobbying complements – rather than competes with – the conventional forms of political participation. If we want to live in a society where policymakers are informed, it is crucial that they have access to accurate, timely and comprehensive information from all sources. Only then can they increase their problem solving capacity and take informed decisions that reflect the public interest. Which means it's up to us to give them that information. Through lobbying, anyone can acquire a political voice, play the political game and influence the democratic process. As the saying goes: if you can't beat 'em, join 'em!

Finally, citizen lobbying enables you to leverage your untapped talents and experiences. Don't be afraid to be creative. The ability to imagine the future is the distinguishing feature of our minds.[27]

Let's take a look at why and how you can do that.

Why Citizen Lobbying?

> 'I asked "Why doesn't somebody do something?"
> Then I realized I was somebody.'
> Anonymous

But you might still be asking why you should embrace citizen lobbying. You may think you have better things to do with your time than meet politicians and civil servants, monitor the policy process and talk to policymakers. But think about how much time you spend talking to your friends about social injustices, sharing news that shocks you on social media or discussing the problems of your lives without even realising that they are shaped – for good or for bad – by policies. By failing to invest time and resources into their root causes, it's no surprise that the democratic system is failing to represent you. How can we tolerate evidence-free, ignorant and sloppy public policy when in our day-to-day jobs we demand skill and rigour? Our whole lives, from the quality of the air we breath, the safety of the food we eat, to the education we provide to our children, are shaped by policies. And as defining these policies has become an ever more demanding, resource-intensive activity – due to the need to take into account more voices and collect more data – your contribution is even more vital than before.

Although it might appear a highly technical exercise, it is time to invest in the policy process. In doing so, you may acquire skills you can use to get a new job or change career, or that will simply make you think differently about your role in society. Indeed, citizen lobbying is not just about informing the policy process and making it more accountable. It also offers you a unique opportunity to use your talents and expertise and to share them for the benefit of society. In a well functioning democracy, the qualities of the citizens matter as much as those of politicians. Last, as previously discussed (see page 4), participating in public life will also contribute to your individual happiness.

By now I hope I have succeeded in demystifying lobbying. And we have already seen its potential to breathe life back into our democracies. Think of how Calvillo and the community of people he successfully mobilised forced the Mexican government to take action against the obesity epidemic affecting the poorest. When Calvillo embarked on his campaign against misleading advertising by soft-drink manufacturers, he invited MPs to meetings led by scientists. They explained that diet was as important as physical activity in preventing obesity. That meeting was a game-changer in the MPs' perception of the problem – and more broadly in their relationship with the citizens. When you lobby as a citizen, you are informing decision-makers and helping them take the public's views into account when they make policy. You can no longer be ignored, especially if your contribution becomes a signal among the noise.

Calvillo's story, and the other stories we looked at in the Introduction, show how citizen lobbyists can – in their spare time – address and break the cycle of powerlessness that entraps us. Power is no longer about assertiveness, dominance and force: it is about making a difference in the world by influencing others.[28]

Let's now examine how citizen lobbying may successfully address the major causes of our growing feeling of powerlessness that we previously identified.

If Nobody Speaks for You, Represent Yourself!

When you lobby as a citizen (you pick a cause and push for it), you fill the 'representation gap' by reaching out to your elected representative and other decision-makers. In particular, by voicing your concerns, you push decision-makers to consider your issue and, eventually, take a stance on it. You can then hold your representative accountable for her actions – or lack thereof.

Lobbying acts as a counterweight to institutionalised power. We could call it counterpower. According to sociologist Manuel Castells' theory of power, counterpower is our capacity to challenge the power embedded in society's institutions so that our values and interests can be represented.[29] In particular, by creating a new space for political reflection and action, citizen lobbying can counter the undue influence of special interests. That's how citizen lobbying contributes to closing the representation gap and making the policy process more equal. Decision-makers start paying attention to opinions and interests they've never listened to before. You have pierced the echo-chamber of politics.

If You're Not in the Club, Tap into Your Own Talent and Expertise!

When acting as a citizen lobbyist you have the opportunity to deploy your own imagination, talent and expertise in the service of an issue you care about. Isn't it about time that you broke out of your job description and offered some of your skills to the rest of society?

It won't be just you who regains control of the policy process and humanises it, but the decision-makers too. Suddenly, you matter to them and they matter to you. Your expertise, leadership, conviction or credibility might even mean they need you. Often citizen lobbyists become the trusted advisors of policymakers, or even companies, that they originally denounced because both parties are able to see the other as a partner rather than an adversary. In a political and civic landscape characterised by passivity, this humanising aspect of citizen lobbying is especially heartening.

If Nobody Teaches You, Learn by Doing!

Acting as a citizen lobbyist entails being exposed to how the system works and learning from it. Fighting for a cause means you develop exactly the skills and attitudes that the policy process needs to survive. Yet not all forms of engagement with the democratic system, whether in a representative or in a more hands-on participatory democracy, necessarily foster a learning experience.[30] For example, a citizen who attended a public hearing or submitted her observations in a public consultation might not learn anything about policymaking.

But citizen lobbyists do more than activating one of the many avenues of participation available to us. They typically enhance civic skills, such as speaking at public meetings, networking and working with others to develop advocacy strategies to accomplish their goals. As a result, acting as a citizen lobbyist sharpens both their individual and our collective democratic understanding. Indeed, a growing body of evidence suggests that citizens who engage with the policy process tend to be more active via conventional political channels.[31] Max Schrems, who was just a student when he took on Facebook, had to educate himself not only about data protection and litigation, but also to learn how the policy process works. Because of that self-education and his struggle to find pro bono lawyers, he also lodged the follow-up suit against Facebook in the Irish courts, alongside citizens willing to help. Max's litigation has inspired many other citizens, both in Europe and in other jurisdictions, to follow suit. As Michael Edwards put it, 'we learn to be citizens not through books or training but through experience and action'.[32]

At a time when so few people understand the political process and inequalities continue to grow steadily, citizen lobbying emerges as a credible approach to reinvigorate citizen engagement, augment social capital and overcome the knowledge gap. Moreover, as Robert Putnam convincingly argued, when people work in social networks and interact with others, their trust of others also increases.[33]

If Somebody Decides for You, Take Back Control!

Lastly, when you become part of and gain a voice in the policy process, you take back control. It is no longer the state or market that decides on your behalf. You are more likely to accept a collective decision that you have had a part in shaping, which means you're more likely to feel a sense of accomplishment, and to have nurtured a feeling of community and joint endeavour.

Time for Citizen Lobbying

> 'Critics of the magistrates are also responsible.
> Their argument is, "The people ought to decide":
> the people accept that invitation readily; and thus
> the authority of the magistrates is undermined.'
> Aristotle, *The Politics*

Contemporary democracy requires minimal public participation – it presents an efficient method of selecting political leaders and putting them to work on policies. However, it fails to encourage and cultivate the social and political skills of each individual, and thus often leaves us feeling disconnected and powerless.[34] Unfortunately, this is also true of many of the petition sites and online calls-to-action that we may turn to in an attempt to engage in civic action. Have you ever asked yourself what happens after you've signed an online petition?

Who does the heavy lifting to explore and execute the petition's demands?

We've already discussed how citizens are spectators, not participants, in the political system and consumers of public policy. This is what civic technology advocate and author Micah Sifry calls 'passive democratic engagement'.[35] However, the marketplace may offer us another model of engagement; in the marketplace, your feedback is often solicited – through customer surveys or requests to leave a product review or rating – and acted upon. But in politics there is no such system for soliciting or offering feedback. Indeed, our offline political systems generally do not even expect any feedback.

The Perils of Direct Democracy

This neglect of public opinion has prompted countless calls for more direct democracy in our systems of government. It is often argued that direct democratic processes, such as referendums and initiatives, give people a better opportunity to speak out than the usual representative processes do. Political leaders, civic advocates and a growing number of citizens portray direct democratic outcomes as the authentic 'voice of the people'. By enabling people to speak directly, without any of the potential distortion inherent in representation, direct democracy seems an irresistible way to respond to the popular will. As a result, the ideal of direct democracy as the expression of popular sovereignty has become a 'quasi-religious commitment' that plays the same role in contemporary democratic ideology as the divine right of kings played in the era of monarchical rule.[36] Why, ask advocates of direct democracy, should we choose a politician to decide for us every few years, if instead we can directly choose the final outcome of a decision and bypass all sorts of personal interests? Can't an individual agree with some measures proposed by a right-wing party and at the same time support some of the ideas of its left-wing opposition? Shouldn't we rely on a referendum to decide every single aspect of our government?

This all sounds exciting and promising, but it entails some major dangers we should bear in mind. First, the voice of the people is not a sufficient condition for democracy, as is frequently implied by the proponents of direct democracy. Government decisions also require the input of experts and, as such, benefit from a plurality of voices. Connected to this point, it seems rather hard to argue that *anything* should be susceptible to a popular vote. Some issues require value judgement and expertise that is difficult to guarantee in a referendum. Third, a major limit of a 'referendum culture' is the perverse incentive to *overvote*, that is, to regulate what doesn't need to be regulated or decided. Finally, direct democracy carries the potential to hurt minority groups insofar as it doesn't accommodate compromise by looking at solutions that are beneficial to all.

As many people have found with recent movements-turned-political parties – Podemos in Spain, the Five Star Movement in Italy and the Pirate parties among them – direct democracy is not in itself a viable response to many of society's challenges. These movements typically determine their official positions by discussing the most relevant issues and elaborating their positions online. Yet not only does the

overall quality of engagement within these self-proclaimed
'direct democracy' experiences remain extremely disappoint-
ing, but their political outcomes don't live up to their rather
idealistic expectations.[37] The base systematically follows the
indications of the vote put forward by its leaders. Uneven
voter turnout, poorly-drafted referendums and the influence
of special interests tend to get in the way of popular input.
Indeed, direct democratic processes *distort* popular input by
preventing people from expressing their priorities.

More importantly, by presenting voters with one issue at a
time, referendums and other forms of direct democracy offer
– as witnessed in the Brexit vote – no opportunity for voters
to channel their political power towards the issues that most
concern them. Giving people the chance to vote 'yes' or 'no' to
this or that particular policy makes people *feel* as though they
have more input, but these kinds of direct democracy actually
limit their ability to influence the overall range of outcomes.
Thus, for instance, after having voted to leave the EU, British
citizens have no voice in determining the new relationship
between their country and the rest of the EU. Yet this is what
will determine the fate of the British economy, the lifestyle of
its people and of future generations.

The most recent experiences of direct democracy suggest
that a political system based on the *unmediated*, constant and
universal participation of all citizens in political matters is not
a realistic option.[38] They remind us that while representative
democracy is not the best way to deliver successful and inclusive political decisions, it is the best way to avoid the 'tyranny
of the majority', a situation in which a temporary majority

changes the rules of the game.[39] Representation typically feels restrictive, but in practice it enables voters to express both single-issue preferences (to recognise same-sex couples or regulate stem cell research, for example) and cross-cutting priorities (e.g. more or less public spending on social welfare).[40]

Numerous experiences suggest that too much reliance on referendums and other instruments of direct democracy may lead the electorate to make self-defeating choices. James Madison made it very clear in *Federalist No. 63* that the defining principle of American democracy, as opposed to Athenian democracy, 'lies in the total exclusion of the people in their collective capacity.'

Because it is so robust and resilient, representative democracy guarantees the vital distinction between those who hold political power (understood as sovereignty) and can legitimately delegate it by voting, and those to whom that power is delegated and who fulfil their mandate by governing transparently and accountably. For this system to work, however, those who hold power must not only control those to whom they have delegated it but must also *connect* with them. That's the weakest link in modern democracies. Besides elections, there is no connection, or next to no connection. The existence of a few online petitions or public consultations ends up making us feel even more powerless by ensuring our engagement is as passive as ever.

So, contrary to what the proponents of direct democracy argue, the challenge ahead is not to *maximise* popular influence in the political process, but to make that influence *more effective* – and meaningful. We should therefore cultivate fewer, not more, participatory opportunities, but render each more meaningful for citizens.

We urgently need innovative forms of participation that can bring us closer to our representatives. Citizen lobbying is a form of engagement that, unlike direct democracy, complements rather than antagonises representative democracy. But like direct democracy, it prods citizens to engage proactively with their elected representatives and their policy and political agendas.

Citizen lobbying is able to provide this missing feedback mechanism and bring it into the policy mainstream. Think about what Zagat does for restaurants, Amazon for books, Uber for transportation, and AirBnB for house-sharing. What these companies have in common is they empower each of us to craft a service according to our preferences, at the exact moment of using the service. Citizen lobbying can do the same for the policy process: offering a trust-based feedback mechanism that can nudge officials to do their jobs better. Designing mechanisms like these demands a deep understanding of the participants' incentives and reputational value, but their purpose is clear: by ensuring quality control, they enhance the accountability of both service provider and user/policymaker and citizen. As Part III explains, some apps – generally tracking systems – allow you to do this more effectively. The UK site Rate Your Politician has allowed its users to rate politicians and policies since 2008. As such the site makes it easy to keep an eye on the UK's parliament by helping people to discover who represents them, how that person has voted and what they've said in debates – simply and clearly.

STORY – The DREAMers

The issue
For the roughly 2 million undocumented citizens living in the United States, it is extremely difficult to obtain the right to reside in the country. The DREAM (Development, Relief, and Education for Alien Minors) Act proposes offering that right to citizens who meet certain qualifications. If the bill passes, up to 850,000 people could benefit.

The action
The bill was first introduced in the Senate in 2001, but has yet to make it through both legislative houses of the US. It was in 2010, following a monumental push from determined activists, that it came closest to doing so. Backing up campaigner Carlos Saavedra's claim that the group would 'put so much pressure on every single senator that is standing between ourselves and our dreams', the group staged high-profile sit-ins in the offices of John McCain and Harry Reid, and supporters made 77,000 phone calls in a single day to senators, urging them to pass the bill. The centrepiece of the demonstrations was a 1,500-mile walk from Miami, Florida, to Capitol Hill in Washington DC, by four students known as the DREAMers.

Mission accomplished?
Not yet. Despite passing through Congress in 2010, the bill was stopped in its tracks shortly afterwards by a filibuster in the Senate. It has failed to make any progress since then.

Does that make it a failure?

After all that effort, they didn't get the bill passed... doesn't that mean citizen lobbying can be a waste of time? No! Despite the obvious disappointment, the activists succeeded in making the plight of the United States' many undocumented citizens a public issue. In 2012 then President Obama announced that his administration would stop deporting young, undocumented citizens who meet certain criteria which were originally proposed by the DREAM Act. But to understand citizen lobbying, we have to look beyond the end result. It goes without saying that the ultimate goal of the DREAMers was to see the bill passed, but the words of the activists themselves show us that the journey they went on personally was equally important. After 'coming out' as an undocumented citizen, Felipe Matos, one of the students who went on the interstate walk, commented: 'I can embrace my struggle in a very public way and I don't have to be scared'. This was echoed by Reyna Wences, who highlighted the liberating nature of the demonstrations: 'There was something about actually coming out and saying it in front of the immigration offices that was so powerful', she said. This is the key message to take from citizen lobbying. Through the fight to create a better world for you and your fellow citizens by playing an active role in the democratic process, you become truer to yourself and closer to the rest of society.

The citizen lobbying road is guaranteed to be lined with positive experiences, whether you achieve your original goal or not.

Let's sum up the case for citizen lobbying.

- At a time of growing demand for direct democracy, citizen lobbying provides an innovative form of citizen participation in the policy process which complements rather than antagonises representative democracy.

- Citizen lobbying creates an additional, permanent channel of contact between elected representatives and electors between elections and, as such, it reconciles protest and proposal.

- In a democracy, public engagement through lobbying broadens the influence people can wield in the policy process and enhances accountability. It makes policymaking better by tapping a bigger reservoir of ideas and resources.[41]

- Citizen lobbying does not just scrutinise government and make it more responsive, but also helps everyone feel (and become) a part of the policy process. It counters the undue influence of special interest groups. Likewise, it challenges the claim of consumer and citizen groups to represent the people, acting as an egalitarian force in society. It helps elected representatives to identify and pursue the public interest. It improves the quality of policymaking while giving all of us a chance to learn about how government works.

- As political narratives and economic and social agendas change across the world, lobbying offers citizens an innovative form of constructive engagement with and influence over the political discourse in our local or national communities. It provides an opportunity to over-come barriers to the acquisition of knowledge produced by growing inequalities.[42]

- Finally, there is a strong correlation between societies characterised by a political culture of critical citizenship – as opposed to allegiant citizenship – and more account-able governments.

It's time we turned the widespread criticisms of politics into an active democratic virtue.

THE TOOL BOX

PART III

THE TOOLBOX

How to Be a Citizen Lobbyist

'Freedom is participation in power.'
Cicero

'Better to die on your feet than to live on your knees.'
Credo of Spanish Civil War

Most of us perceive the world of lobbying as mysterious and uninviting. Some are even afraid of it, as if lobbying were taboo. Yet we have just seen how it can help us make a difference to our lives. Indeed, lobbying is one of the most effective yet least understood ways of taking control of our lives. First, it enables each of us to realise our untapped talents, expertise and passion. Then it lets us channel these resources into the causes we feel most deeply about in order to bring about change. Finally, it boosts our individual and collective wellbeing thanks to the positive correlation between engagement and happiness.

Never has there been a better time to start experimenting with citizen lobbying. More and more democracies are throwing open the policy process to citizens as they recognise the need for more inclusive decision-making.[1] Novel forms of public participation and engagement are emerging that are opening up new ways for citizens to get involved.[2]

It's time to seize your power as a citizen and learn how to use it in your daily life. That's the purpose of Part III.

Some of the questions I hear most often are:

- When is it best to remain low-key rather than going public?

- When do you push for a face-to-face meeting, send emails and/or launch a digital campaign?

- When do you need scientific studies for evidence as opposed to symbolic arguments?

- How do you decide whether to team up with somebody else?

Before we open the 'citizen lobbying toolbox' to address these queries, let's get something straight. Firstly, there is no one-size-fits-all method for successful lobbying. There is no such a thing as the best advocacy strategy, the best lobbying avenue, the best tactic; successful lobbying must be tailored to the situation in hand. Lobbying is a plunge into deep waters, and, while we can always learn diving technique from others, how we execute those techniques will vary based on different conditions and on our own abilities. Since political agendas and processes alter over time, the tools, techniques and tactics of lobbying have to change as well. Lobbying has to be context-specific. This is not to say that it cannot be taught – but lobbying must be understood as an adaptive *process*, or a set of steps that we need to follow in order to influence policy outcomes.[3]

Three main factors shape the lobbying game:

1. the nature of the issue at stake (e.g. animal welfare, nuclear energy or LGBT rights);

2. the constitutional and institutional setting (e.g. who is competent to act? The city council, an international organisation or the Prime Minister's Office) and

3. special interest groups (who wins and who loses from each outcome and their respective influence).

These three factors determine how you should tailor the lobbying plan, avenues of action, arguments, tactics and alliances. It's important to get the mix right.

In order to bring about change, any lobbying plan must also be frequently reassessed – together with its tactics, messaging and overall understanding of the lobbying environment – so that it remains relevant. Contrary to what you might have heard, lobbying is not about taking decision-makers out for expensive dinners and offering them gifts. Nor is it just sending a few emails or even launching a digital campaign; these will not necessarily be enough to make your lobbying effort a success. Lobbying is more than just spending time with decision-makers; it requires the ability to understand the dynamics governing policymaking, its actors and processes as well as what makes the media tick. And it requires a lot of rigorous research work so you can demonstrate the empirical evidence backing up your recommendations and provide facts that show they are viable. Lobbying demands the ability to communicate to multiple audiences and know what those audiences need and expect. Often it requires mobilising some public support – through, for instance, grassroots activism.

In short, lobbying is what feeds the little-known but powerful world of policymaking. By bringing fresh ideas, data and energy to the policy process, it pumps blood into the veins of the political system.

Citizen lobbying is no exception. Like other kinds of lobbying, it requires a context-specific, evidence-based approach if it is to persuade decision-makers. It is the process by which citizens get organised, formulate arguments, identify targets, select tactics and decide whether to work with others in an attempt to influence public policy, thus improving their daily lives.

The 10-Step Citizen Lobbying Guide

The 10-step framework that follows will help you devise a successful lobbying strategy. We will then explore how to execute each step in further detail.

This is a comprehensive plan of action to guide and empower citizen lobbyists. It's practical but leaves you a lot of room for creative thinking and adaptation.

1. **Pick your battle**. The list of possible issues is pretty much infinite. How do you choose yours? Techniques such as monitoring and issue identification (which we'll discuss shortly) can help, but co-generation of ideas within your community is key. To succeed you need to be as passionate as you are strategic about your issue.

2. **Do your homework**. Any lobbying action requires some research work. Your research should generally focus on hard facts, figures and data. Expert and authoritative sources will help to back up your position. They must first be summed up in a background document and then distilled into a single-page factsheet that explains why the issue matters, at what level(s) of government it may be addressed, how you propose to solve it, why the solution will work – and, ideally, how your solution(s) work elsewhere around the world. You'll need this evidence not only to convince others, but also to structure your mind

around an issue you feel passionately about. Your home-work will help you keep your cool and give you credibility in front of audiences that may want to try to make you look foolish.

3. **Map your lobbying environment**. Before you design your lobbying strategy, you need to draw a map that shows who your possible allies and opponents are. This map will be a working tool that allows you to identify:

   a. the lobbying target (e.g. relevant policymakers);

   b. people you might work with (e.g. allies);

   c. your opponents (in order to anticipate their arguments and avoid traps).

   Knowing who these groups are will be key to preparing the answers that will be expected from you during the lobbying.

4. **Draw up a lobbying plan**. Once you know what you're going to lobby for, and with whom, you need to devise a comprehensive lobbying strategy. This means identifying the best course(s) of action to take in order to make your case. Should you engage in *inside lobbying* (directed at political parties and government) or *outside lobbying* (targeted at the general public and media)? Should you concentrate on formal or unconventional kinds of engagement and influence? (You can of course combine both.) Be aware that your choice of action and tactics will

determine virtually all the ensuing steps, from branding and coalition-building to communication and funding.

5. **Pick your allies**. Once you have your map, you can work out whom to encourage to join your cause. Generally, the broader-based your coalition, the greater the chance you have of attracting the attention of policymakers. Be open-minded: it isn't just non-profit organisations that can be brought on board. Companies can too, if they will add value without questioning the legitimacy of your plans. You might even find that your most obvious allies, such as the NGOs active in your field, are not necessarily ready to team up with you.

6. **Raise money.** Citizen lobbying does not necessarily require funding. Yet, while volunteering can work wonders, you might still have costs to meet. Depending on the nature, scope and extent of the action, you could need help from friends and family, and perhaps some seed capital, to cover some of the expenses you might encounter. Putting together a campaign plan and estimating the costs for each element will give you a clearer sense of your fundraising goal. Don't be afraid or ashamed to ask for money; people will respond if you let your passion and belief shine through.

7. **Plan your communication.** Lobbying involves communicating with at least three different audiences: policymakers, the general public and the media. Depending on your

lobbying strategy you must work out how and when to talk, and to whom. Sometimes you must also determine who speaks on behalf of your issue.

8. **Face-to-face meetings.** Meeting face-to-face with policymakers is the essence of citizen lobbying. It is not just desirable but often vital for your campaign. These meetings are your opportunity to connect with the decision-makers, and their chance to listen to you and learn about your cause. You need to make sure you are fully prepared, even if you only end up talking to an assistant! You will need to know how to introduce yourself and 'speak the language' (the talking points) that the decision-maker uses.

9. **Monitor progress and delivery.** You may have managed to 'sell' your issue to one or more policymakers who will promote it through the political process, but that's not the end. You need to remain vigilant and help them to make sure that your cause will advance.

10. **Stick to lobbying rules.** During your campaign, you must keep an eye on the law. What can and can't you do? The good news is that as a citizen you are not only entitled to lobby any public official, but you are also free to do so without automatically being subject to the rules governing professional lobbying.

To make the presentation of each step tangible and salient with you, the next sections of the book will be referring to my past and on-going advocacy campaigns. In particular, I will make reference to a campaign – co-created with an academic colleague – aimed at restricting the marketing of alcohol in Europe.

STORY – Alcohol Marketing Restrictions

Who hasn't longed for a glass of French wine, or a fresh Belgian beer? Alcohol is more than a marketable product for most Europeans: it is part of their history and their culture. The European Union has the highest rate of alcohol consumption in the world – 10.2 litres of pure alcohol per person per year.

Yet alcohol presents dangers of which many Europeans seem unaware. It has been recognised by the World Health Organisation to be the third leading risk factor for disease and mortality in Europe. In 2015, alcohol was responsible for one in seven male deaths and one in thirteen female deaths in the 15–64 age group in Europe. In other words, 120,000 people died prematurely due to alcohol in 2015. Moreover, alcohol marketing has become more aggressive in recent years, targeting the European youth in particular.

In order to reduce excessive consumption of alcohol, Amandine Garde (University of Liverpool) and I have promoted a European Citizens' Initiative (ECI) project aimed at drafting a directive to regulate alcohol marketing in the EU.

One million signatures then need to be collected over a twelve month period, across seven Member States. This will allow the project to be submitted to the European Commission for consideration.

There is an actual demand for such an ECI among European citizens. According to the Eurobarometer survey, three quarters of the EU population (76 per cent), would approve the banning of alcohol advertising targeting young people in all member states, with every second respondent (50 per cent) answering that they 'agree totally' with this idea. A country-by-country analysis shows that in all countries the majority of respondents would favour such a ban, the strongest support (93 per cent) being seen in Slovakia (with 68 per cent 'totally agreeing'), and less support in Luxembourg (58 per cent, with 41 per cent 'totally agreeing') and Denmark (59 per cent, with 37 per cent 'totally agreeing').

Before moving on, let's see if you are ready. Here are some questions to help you identify where you currently stand:

- Are you sure – based on your direct experience or preliminary research – that your issue won't be tackled unless you take action?

- Do you feel capable and ready to carry it through?

- Do you have enough enthusiasm and energy to last what could be a long journey?

- Are you ready to learn the tools that power citizen lobbying?

If you answered yes to these questions now, or after reading the rest of this book, then you are ready to become a citizen lobbyist and start planning your campaign.

Now you know the main steps of successful citizen advo-cacy and you seem ready to go, let's explore them one by one. They are presented in logical order, so you might want to follow them step-by-step. Avoid treating them as a checklist, though: you must revisit each step as you work through the process.

We are now ready to examine the first step in our list: pick your battle.

STEP 1: Pick Your Battle

> 'The best way to predict your future is to create it.'
> Abraham Lincoln

The first step is to know what you want. What do you want to change? This is what we call 'issue identification', or – in activ-ists' language – the *battle*. The list of issues you might want to address is virtually infinite. No policy is ever perfected. Choosing your battle is not necessarily the result of a rational process – it can emerge when you suddenly feel that you must stand up – but you can still think strategically before acting.

Climate change policy, action to protect bees, LGBT rights, admission policy to your local school, whistle-blower protection: almost anything you deem worthwhile can be brought to policymakers' attention. It might be local, national or even have an international dimension.

The range of issues at stake may feel overwhelming. But don't worry – you don't have to come up with an original idea to become a successful citizen lobbyist. You may pick up an idea you came across in conversation with friends, family or colleagues, in an op-ed piece or on a blog. That's where most of my best ideas for new citizen campaigns come from!

The more the ideas are generated by yourself, friends and colleagues, on the basis of a shared experience, the more representative, enthusiastic and promising your project will be. In other words, stick to reality.

Although you can pick virtually any issue that concerns you, your choice needs to be strategic. There is a big difference between lobbying on an issue that is already being discussed by the media and politicians, and lobbying on an issue that you have to sell from scratch. While the latter scenario is obviously more challenging and demanding, your action – if successful – could be even more impactful. You will be the one framing the debate!

A number of tools can help you monitor what is going on in the policy space. And since timing is key when it comes to influencing any process, you really want to be first so that the conversation is anchored to your point of view and concerns. Professional lobbyists call this monitoring. Most countries publish online legislative initiatives – generally called 'bills' – at a local and national level. In the UK, the key monitoring tool is called Hansard. The US has THOMAS, the Library of Congress website, which tracks federal legislation in action. The EU has Eur-lex. Almost every country has its own monitoring tools.

Monitoring tools also help you find out the major actors involved in an initiative. Bills in the US are sponsored by congressmen. In the UK any Member of Parliament can introduce a bill. Some bills represent agreed government policy, and are introduced into Parliament by ministers; all others are known as private members' bills. A similar system applies in most of the world. In the EU, legislative proposals always come from the European Commission, and only then they are entrusted to a Member of the European Parliament (MEP), generally called a rapporteur.

Various media outlets track the progress of major policy initiatives, such as *Politico* (both in the US and Europe), *The Hill* and *Euractiv*; plus, there are other national counterparts. Often they offer free email newsletters to which you can subscribe.

Alongside these conventional information channels, you can often follow the progress of legislation on social media. Public officials run personal websites and circulate newsletters, and their offices and organisations do the same; you can keep up to date with them through an RSS feed. Many news sites, blogs and other online publishers syndicate their content in this format to deliver fresh content. Monitoring these sites will help you find out about policy decisions, new issues and debates before the general public does.

Unlike previous generations, you have Google. On top of using basic and advanced searches, you can also set up Google Alerts for free and receive email notifications whenever Google finds new results on a topic that interests you. For example, you could get updates about a cause you like, or discover immediately when something about you pops up on the web. Over the years, this has been the most effective and inexpensive monitoring tool I've used.

Last but not least, never forget that your own community is a great place to identify, detect and understand live issues. In other words: leave the office, break the silence and talk to people! Doing your work in a café, as most of my fellow citizen lobbyists do, makes this easier. Amid the urge to act, don't forget that talking to others is one of the best ways to explore your ideas, test your plans and find out whether they make sense before you put them into practice. This is what we call 'talking with purpose'. Having said that, never forget that you can't listen if you are too busy talking. Listening teaches you just as much as talking does. Moreover, by empathising with others, as you do when you listen properly, you'll gain a huge advantage with policymakers once you start discussing the same issues with them.

'Easy Wins' and Other Good Starting Places

Some issues are inevitably easier to sell than others – either because of their inherent nature, or the spirit of the times. For example, efforts to limit individual choice – typically in an effort to crack down on alcohol or tobacco use, or gambling – are likely to meet resistance. The more socially acceptable it is to behave in a particular way, the tougher you will find it to argue for change. Conversely, issues on which public opinion is already starting to change, such as same-sex relationships or cannabis use, might be easier to tackle. Here are a few relatively easy wins.

The 'Revolving Door'

This is about public officials who leave office to take on

corporate posts, making money out of the connections and influence they acquired in office. The risk that these people may undermine democratic decision-making is high.[4] Imagine that an outgoing regulator joins the very same bank that she has previously been regulating. The key strength of this battle is that very few people, except maybe the ex-politicians concerned, would dare to openly defend the revolving door phenomenon. Even indifference would go down badly. How could you consider it to be a healthy relationship between the public and the private sectors? If you find the right way to go about it, you can quickly gather huge support. That's why the petition launched on WeMove.eu after former EU Commissioner President Barroso took a job at Goldman Sachs gathered 100,000+ signatures within a few days.

Data Protection

Data protection issues, such as how to protect your data when it is collected and traded among businesses, is set to inspire a large number of citizen actions. In the space of just six years, privacy has become a core issue that attracts substantial financial backing — shown, for example, not just by the recent surge of mainstream privacy start-ups such as Sirin Labs,[5] but also by the $250m bankrolling of *The Intercept* magazine, which aims to hold governments and businesses to account, while doggedly protecting the security and anonymity of its sources. Activist groups, non-profits and NGOs have never experienced such a boost in popularity and funds.[6] These campaigners are building a new framework of strategic activism that aims to create reputational damage by destabilising public confidence in targeted companies.

Drones
Although countries like the UK already have some drone legislation in place, it is proving difficult to prosecute people for crimes such as flying them too close to buildings or people, or in crowded areas. Commercial airline pilots have also reported drones being flown close to airports. Their growing popularity and availability present several dangers that may call for legislation.

Drug Monopolies
A number of pharmaceutical firms have come under fire in recent years for charging extortionate prices for drugs over which they enjoy a monopoly. A notable example is Turin Pharmaceuticals, a start-up run by a former hedge fund manager, which in 2015 acquired Daraprim – a drug used to treat HIV – and immediately increased its price by more than 5,000 per cent.[7] This brought the annual cost of treatment for some patients to hundreds of thousands of dollars.

Big Pharma Under-reporting
AllTrials is a project countering the phenomenon of under-reporting of clinical trials by advocating that clinical research adopts the principles of open research. The project summarises itself as 'All trials registered, all results reported': that is, all clinical trials should be listed in a registry and their results should always be shared as open data. At the heart of

the organisation is a petition signed by over 85,000 individuals and 599 organisations. As of today, thousands of clinical trials have not reported their results; some have not even been registered. Information on what was done and what was found in these trials could be lost forever to doctors and researchers, leading to bad treatment decisions, missed opportunities for good medicine and trials being repeated. All trials past and present should be registered, and the full methods and results reported.

Sustainable Development Goals (SDGs)

A unique opportunity to test citizen lobbying is offered by the implementation of Sustainable Development Goals (SDGs). Despite their pretty unattractive name, these were agreed by UN Member States in September 2015 as the successor framework to the Millennium Development Goals (MDGs). The SDGs are a new, universal set of goals, targets and indicators that UN Member States will be expected to use to frame their agendas and public policies over fifteen years (2015–30). With seventeen goals and 169 targets covering the social, economic and environmental spheres, the SDGs are part of the '2030 Agenda for Sustainable Development'. While the MDGs were aimed at developing countries, the SDGs are universal, apply to all countries and foresee an active engagement of civil society to actually attain them. The goals embrace and reflect the interconnectedness of social, economic and environmental challenges and, most importantly, reflect a powerful aspiration to improve our world – laying out where we collectively and individually need to go and how to get there.

Citizen lobbyists will be essential – together with political, business and civic leaders – to achieve this transformational change. While not legally binding, as an internationally-agreed policy framework, governments will be encouraged to demonstrate progress against the goals and targets on the international stage. Against this backdrop, citizens are expected to play a key role in engaging with all relevant actors and to pressurise their governments to deliver on their pledges.

Do you have a realistic chance of success? Since organising is hard work and generally involves roping in various people, you probably want to be sure that your plan has a real chance of success. Of course, this doesn't mean you shouldn't embark on a plan unless you can come up with a winning tactic. Most of the time, you need to score a series of small victories to create the momentum that will lead to success.

The final element to consider – and this is the ultimate test – is how passionate you are about the issue. Citizen lobbying is something you do alongside your main job, so you need a real passion for it. Ask yourself if this is the issue you're going to make time for.

ACTIVITY 1 – Chart the Issue and its Solutions

Now that you know how to pick up an issue you feel deeply about, grab a pen and notebook, laptop, iPad or (even better) a flipchart or board. Write down a brief statement describing what you are concerned about ('the issue') and start thinking what to do about it ('the solutions').

We'll get into more detail on creating solutions shortly, but for now it's valuable to think about the problem and its solutions in tandem. Do it now, and keep these statements updated as you monitor the issues, talk to people and share ideas with friends and colleagues.

Situating the Issue

Once you have identified your cause (or causes), you need to find out whether it has already entered the policy process via a policy proposal, resolution or even an international treaty. Then identify which stage it has reached. Is the issue due for a hearing or vote? Does a proposal already exist or has the issue already been addressed by a new regulation that you dislike? Is it part of an administrative process?

In order to avoid getting bogged down, you need some benchmarks. The diagram on the next page is a very simple visualisation of the policy cycle that I came up with a few years ago and regularly use in my own work and teaching. It shows the process by which new initiatives are adopted, and can help you to figure out how far policy has already progressed on your issue by the time you join in.

The policy process typically includes the major phases shown below the diagram.

As a citizen lobbyist, you may get involved with one or more of the phases. You might draw policymakers' attention to your cause and provide data and statistics to understand it (problem definition), come up with ideas for solving it (consultation and design of policy options), influence the enactment (adoption and implementation), and even go as

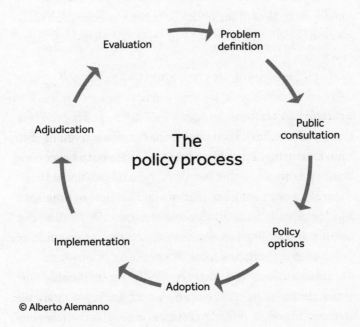

© Alberto Alemanno

1. Problem definition: what the issue is

2. Public consultation: what people think about the issue

3. Design of the policy options: how to solve the issue

4. Adoption: making a decision to adopt the solution

5. Policy implementation: the implementation of the solution

6. Policy adjudication: somebody may challenge the solution(s) before the Courts

7. Policy evaluation: how well the solution worked.

far as to challenge the final policy outcome (adjudication) if you dislike it. Should the policy be subject to evaluation (policy evaluation), you may want to seize this chance to shape its revision.

But if the issue you are promoting is not yet on policymakers' radar, your lobbying journey will have to start earlier. The first challenge will be to get your issue into the policy cycle (via problem definition). Promoting a solution for something that is not yet deemed a problem could turn out to be initially more challenging than one that has already gained public attention.

Sometimes your issue may not call for new or amended laws, but simply an administrative decision. This will be the case if you want public authorities to stop the construction of a mall or to authorise a protest, for example. In this situation, you need to understand the process leading up to the adoption of that decision. In other circumstances, your aim might be even more modest. What you seek is for decision-makers to take a stance upon a particular societal issue, such as domestic violence or same-sex relationships, so as to prompt a change in social perception.

ACTIVITY 2 – Map Your Issue

Now that you have picked your battle, chart it in the right spot in the policy process cycle. Is it a new idea? Or is it a pending initiative you want to promote or stop? Find out where your initiative stands before you pick it, and then chart its possible steps.

STEP 2: Do Your Homework

> 'We need to first define the problem. If I had an hour
> to save the world I would spend 59 minutes defining
> the problem and one minute finding solutions.'
> Albert Einstein

Any lobbying action requires some background research work, regardless of its complexity.

Firstly, no matter how brilliant your proposed solution might be, it alone will not be enough to persuade policymakers to adopt it. Do you want to block the construction of a nuclear plant? Do you want to get an LGBT rights law on the statute book? Do you want to protect whistle-blowers? To pursue any of these causes, you will generally be expected to speak the language of policymakers: hard facts, figures and data. You'll need arguments backed up by data in order to build your case for action. Usually, these will come from expert and authoritative sources backing up your position. If you neglect to educate yourself about the issue, or are so hasty in your research that you misinterpret or misrepresent information, you're doomed to failure. What credibility can you possibly inspire in a decision-maker if you can't prove that you know your facts?

Secondly, by going through the research process you'll start meeting your lobbying allies, and only then will you really realise what it takes to get a citizen lobbying action off the ground. While you can go it alone, you may want to consider sharing your journey with someone else. Indeed, you will probably need a core team to challenge you to understand the issue properly, and to come up with a convincing solution. Your core team will also help you master the steps ahead. By thinking collectively, we create the right conditions to gather knowledge and act.[8] Genuine dialogue transforms the quality of conversation and the thinking that lies behind it. As we'll see on page 154, you first need to draw up a fully-fledged citizen lobbying plan which sets out the avenues and tactics you are going to deploy. Then you need to carry it out.

Thirdly, no citizen lobbying should be limited to a search for a political solution. Instead, it should aim to bring about a deeper change of attitude and perception. There is always a risk that without public support a policy change may not survive (or even be implemented at all). Smoking does not instantly become less popular through banning it. It is when the social norms around smoking change that people quit. A campaign to introduce restrictions on smoking in public spaces might bring this about because it makes lighting up less socially acceptable.

All these elements – speaking the language of policy-makers, setting up a core team and changing public attitudes – make it crucial that you gather evidence before racing ahead with your plan.

The success of your lobbying will largely depend on the quality of your initial research work. Good research leads to informed strategies (Step 4 of the citizen lobbying framework), effective branding/communication (Step 7), exhaustive mapping (Step 3), as well as to smart coalition building (Step 5). At the same time, going through each of the following steps will call for further research – and this will feed back into your existing work, informing your overall lobbying strategy. Research is an ongoing task. Be sure to integrate it into your overall lobbying strategy.

ACTIVITY 3 – Prepare a Background Document

You've already identified the issue you want to work on and a possible solution (or set of solutions). Collect this first set of ideas, including the chart and its institutional implications, into a background document that you and your team will update. This will consist of bullet points summing up your major findings. To make collaborative drafting easier, create a shared document (e.g. Google Drive, Dropbox, etc.).

Is Your Issue a Real Issue?

The first goal of your research phase is to sound out your issue with people outside of close family, friends and colleagues. Before becoming an advocate for any cause, you need to be sure that someone else feels the same so that you aren't advocating for a change that no one else wants. To what extent do other people perceive your issue as a problem? If you can't find anyone who seems to care about it much, then be ready to look a bit wider for potential supporters. This reality check is the best antidote against 'groupthink'. This occurs when a group's need for consensus supersedes the judgement of individual group members. Groupthink generally occurs when there is a time constraint and individuals put aside personal doubts so a project can move forward. Sometimes it is prompted by someone in the group dominating the decision-making process.

To be successful, you need to find people who can see your issue from different perspectives. Don't be afraid of disagreement; the aim is not to find a consensus, but simply to test whether other people perceive the issue in a similar way, even though they might have different ideas about it. The sooner you discover this, the better. You don't want to go into battle for a cause that's doomed to failure.

TIP 1 – Pitch Your Issue

Don't be afraid to be creative when testing your idea beyond your friends and contacts.

Think about recording a short video and circulating it on social media and YouTube to avoid the echo chambers of your like-minded friends. The feedback you get – in the forms of likes and/or comments – will help you understand whether your issue is of concern to other people and why. Another more conventional but still effective way is to write a letter or op-ed for a newspaper, local or national, to flag up an issue and attract supporters. You'll be surprised at how many people contact you wanting to help and even to team up with you!

Team Building

The next phase of your research focuses on gathering facts and supporters. You need to build a case. For this, you need a core team of people willing to run and dig in on the project. Consider assigning tasks to different people who know the issue inside out – whether they are classmates, colleagues, friends or people you don't know yet. Are there individuals, groups and other organisations already campaigning on the issue? Or are there existing citizens' groups, non-profits or other organisations that have already produced research on your issue? You might have come across some of them during the previous, identification phase. They might have enjoyed talking to you, they might have heard about your plans and some may even have contacted you. Unlike you, citizens' groups or other organisations generally have dedicated staff and funding. So if they embrace – or at least support – your cause, your chances of success increase. While it might be premature at this stage of your project to design a coalition (this will come up during Step 5), you could start preparing the ground for one. As I've already mentioned, the ten steps are often interrelated and may need to be undertaken out of a strictly chronological order.

These serendipitous encounters with other organisations, activists, academics and experts can turn out to be incredibly powerful, as they often make the difference between failure and success. It is only when you start scratching the surface of your initiative that you meet your allies – and find out what it takes to get your citizen lobbying action off the ground.

Be bold when you seek out people who will share your passion for the issue and want to help out. Think about calling a meeting, even if you don't know whether anyone will show up. Rely on social media, such as Facebook, to circulate the call and then, if you can't meet face-to-face, you can host it for free on Skype or as a Google Hangout. The online platform Meetup could help you plan an event like this, especially if you want it to take place in different venues across the world. Once the meeting is convened, you'll need to introduce the issue, collect participants' names and contact information, propose a brief round in which everyone introduces themselves and eventually chair a brainstorming session about what to do.

Without killing the spontaneity of the gathering, the brainstorm should be structured along a few simple lines, such as:

i.   What is the issue?
ii. What do we want to do about it?
iii. Who will do what?
iv. What skills do we have internally?
v.   What do we need and who could help?
vi. What is the timeline?

Regardless of whether you agree with your new colleagues or not (on the problem and/or the many other items that come up), your understanding of the issue and ability to think strategically about what to do will improve. This meeting might be the start (or indeed the end) of your citizen lobbying initiative.

Gather Your Facts

Once you've established an initial core team willing to dig into the issue, it's time to move on to the next phase of your research. This focuses on collecting the facts documenting the issue and supporting your proposed solution. In particular, you must gather evidence on these three crucial areas, bearing in mind the following questions:

- Evidence on the issue: Why does this issue matter?

- Evidence on the solution: What do you propose and why will it work?

- Evidence on the precedents: How has your solution already worked elsewhere?

TIP 2 – Work as a Network and Be Agile

As soon as the core group emerges, make sure you capitalise on your first brainstorming session and move the conversation to a dedicated platform. While basic email and Skype may serve their purpose at the beginning, they will soon become too cumbersome to use in daily life. My advice – based on experience of citizen lobbying – is to use closed online communities, such as a dedicated Facebook group or, even better, Slack. Slack is a program that allows your team to export information to a chat app, such as WhatsApp; it also enables you to create thematic channels and share files.

While it's a good idea to try to meet face-to-face once in a while, don't waste time looking for an office space; you can work from home or in a café and meet others in public places, or online. If you can't meet up in person, keep your Skype or Google Hangout open while everyone is working on the project from their own corner of the world.

Lack of resources means citizen lobbyists can rarely compete with the professionals when it comes to gathering evidence. But that doesn't mean you should cut corners. Ensure that your work complies as much as possible with reliable research methods so as to avoid a challenge later in the process. If you don't know how to conduct desk research (gathering and analysing information already available in print or published on the internet) or run a survey, you may want to rely on someone who does to help you design your research work.

Experts may, however, be beyond your budget. A way to get around that is to rely on experts who volunteer, providing research 'pro bono' – professional work undertaken without payment and for the public good.

Don't be afraid to drop an email to an academic or an expert consultant who has been writing about or working on your issue. They might volunteer to share some of their knowledge with you. If some of them are like me (and I know they are!), they might even take up your cause. I regularly receive all sorts of queries from people across the world who are looking for help on both substantive and procedural aspects of their citizen battles. Because I find it very rewarding as an academic to share my expertise and support their causes, I generally agree to do so on a pro bono basis.

While the idea of pro bono has always existed, in particular among lawyers, a global pro bono movement has recently emerged. All kinds of professionals – graphic designers, communications specialists, accountants, business students and many more (including carpenters, plumbers and other trades) are dedicating a portion of their time and labour unpaid to help NGOs working for social causes. Their volunteering might be in the form of writing a business plan, drafting a press release or running a social media campaign. The key is to channel individuals' skills and talents towards causes they believe in. In the US, the skill-based volunteering movement is in full swing, pioneered by organisations like the Taproot Foundation, which makes business talent available to NGOs (of which my organisation, The Good Lobby, is a global fellow); Pro Bono Net and Appleseed, which enable lawyers to both volunteer their expertise to individuals in need of advice, and to work on broader social justice initiatives; Datakind, which engages data science experts on projects addressing critical humanitarian problems; and the St. Bernard Project, which enlists tradesmen to rebuild houses for disaster victims. Some corporations have even been willing to use their public affairs departments to lobbying for good.[9] If you're interested in finding out more about any of these organisations, you can find further information and links at the end of the book.

In Europe, the movement has been patchier, but it is gaining momentum fast. In the legal field PILnet was an early player, linking lawyers all across Europe with not-for-profit organisations (NPOs) in need of legal support. National organisations providing a similar service have sprung up – like aadh in France and Centrum Pro Bono in Poland. Beyond law, organisations dedicated to enabling all kinds of business professionals and academics to volunteer their skills are emerging in Germany (Proboneo), Spain (Fundación Hazloposible), France (pro bono lab) and Poland (Fundacja Dobra Sieć). In the Netherlands, a highly innovative project was launched as long ago as 1996: Beursvloer. It is an annual 'marketplace' (or stock exchange) where companies, volunteer organisations and local authorities can meet and build partnerships, matching supply and demand.

Be aware that some pro bono volunteers who are actively looking for projects might be willing to join your core team.

TIP 3 – The Power of Pro Bono

Don't be afraid to knock on doors (well, write emails!) when looking for independent experts. The more open you are about your issue, the more likely you are to attract them. Personal relationships and word-of-mouth work marvellously when amplified by social networks. Plus, today there are plenty of matchmaking platforms, often called clearinghouses, which connect experts with causes. In particular, you may want to check The Good Lobby, the organisation I co-founded.

ACTIVITY 4 – Look for a Pro Bono Matching Platform

As the number of skill-volunteering platforms continues to grow, make sure to identify them to be connected with experts on your cause. Check out the organisations we've just talked about and those listed in Resources section.

Evidence on the Issue

The first type of evidence you need is about the nature, extent and salience of the issue you have chosen. In other words, why has your issue become an issue? Why does it call for action? If you are lobbying against smoking, you'll probably focus first on showing the scientific evidence proving it harms health, then will determine how many premature deaths are due to tobacco. If you lobby for LGBT rights, your evidence will focus on proving that, without legal protection, discrimination occurs – listing how often, and how badly. If you lobby against fracking, you must prove its negative environmental consequences. If you oppose the construction of a nuclear plant in your area, you must demonstrate the environmental and health dangers it will cause.

Most of this evidence is widely available and can be easily gathered via desk (also known as secondary) research. This is the summary, collation and/or synthesis of existing research. As research findings are increasingly (yet still not universally) 'open access', they are often freely available online. Sometimes, however, the evidence you need is not easy to grab from the web – and sometimes it doesn't exist at all. That's usually because your cause is relatively new. Let's suppose that you're the mother of a teenager who was killed by a car while playing Pokémon Go, the first location-based, augmented reality game. You will need to prove the negative consequences for society of playing this game – well beyond your own anecdotal evidence.

In these circumstances, you need to get out and produce the information yourself. This is generally referred to as primary research, i.e. data that is collected from, for example, research subjects or experiments. This may mean using techniques such as surveys, focus groups or door-to-door questioning. You might survey neighbours, students or colleagues to verify how many of them are facing (or feeling strongly about) your issue. These techniques may be demanding and time consuming. They therefore often require the involvement of experts, who might agree to work on a pro bono basis.

When discussing evidence in the policy process, it is crucial to distinguish between evidence on the causes of problems (e.g. smoking) and evidence on the solutions to those problems (i.e. policy interventions aimed at tackling smoking). The former refers to the causal link between a suggested risk factor – such as tobacco, discrimination, fracking or playing Pokémon Go – and an undesirable outcome, such as illness, exclusion from opportunities open to the majority, poisoning or premature death. The latter, evidence on solutions, refers instead to the potential of different policy interventions (also called policy options) to reduce harm or promote a positive outcome. These might be a prohibition on indoor smoking, a ban on fracking or a restriction on the use of Pokémon Go.

Providing evidence about the nature and/or extent of the issue you want public authorities to tackle may turn out to be quite demanding. This is all the truer when the phenomenon you're worried about is relatively new, as novelty may explain the lack of empirical data. How can you prove that there are sufficient negative consequences from playing Pokémon Go to warrant restrictions? Did the game lead to higher mortality rates among teenagers in its first year of existence? Often phenomena are multifactorial (caused by several factors) and as such are complex to fully grasp. Think about obesity: it results from the combination of several dynamics – excessive eating, genetic make-up, brain-reward mechanisms and socio-economic factors – which all have different explanations. Furthermore, as many factors may contribute to a given condition, a causal link may be impossible to establish reliably. For example, how many injuries are caused by Pokémon Go as opposed to texting or the use of other apps? How many car accidents are directly 'caused by' alcohol? To what extent is obesity caused by advertising foods that are high in fat, sugar or salt? Any form of public intervention that you advocate has to acknowledge this complexity.

TIP 4 – Give Your Issue a Human Face

Never forget that abstract figures proving the existence of your issue are not enough. When you gather evidence, make sure you meet people who have been directly affected by the issue you're concerned about. Their stories will give your campaign a human face: only when we hear their stories will we realise why that issue matters and think 'that could have been me'. Don't hesitate to get quotes from people (even anonymous ones if they don't feel comfortable about revealing their identity). They speak volumes.

Evidence on the Solution

Once you've established the nature, extent and overall salience of the issue you want to tackle, you must focus on your proposed solution. You need to demonstrate why what you're asking decision-makers to do is the way forward. No matter how brilliant your proposed solution, you need to prove to decision-makers that it might actually work. In the past, policy decisions were often taken on the basis of anecdotal evidence and ideology, or simply at random. Today policy-making tends be more informed. Most countries now prepare impact assessment studies on their policy initiatives. These documents provide a detailed and systematic appraisal of the potential impacts of a new policy initiative in order to assess whether it will have the desired effect and whether bringing about some good in one field may inflict proportionally greater damage in another.

These studies generally compare different solutions in order to identify the one that works best. The idea is to ensure that regulation will enhance society's overall wellbeing. In particular, a growing number of countries, including the United States, Japan and most European countries, establish whether a proposed action will bring in more benefits than costs (cost-benefit analysis) before they enact it. This approach converts all the costs and benefits of your proposed solution into a monetary metric and then measures the two. How can you define a 'benefit to society' and defend it?

To be able to subject your solution to a cost-benefit analysis, you need to collect data proving the effectiveness of your solution when compared with the status quo and/or other solutions. From a health perspective, is it more effective to ban indoor smoking, or to levy a tobacco tax? From an environmental perspective, is it more effective to ban coal plants or fracking? Can you weigh up the health and environmental harm caused by coal combustion fumes with the potential fall in GDP caused by the difficulty in replacing coal as a power source?

Generally, it is more difficult to gather evidence supporting your proposed action – be it a ban, a restriction or total opposition to an initiative – than to prove the existence of the underlying issue you want to address. This is for a multitude of reasons. Firstly, there is generally more evidence available about the underlying problem (smoking) than about its possible solutions (taxation increase, indoor ban, warnings). These solutions, including yours, tend to be either untried or context-specific (an indoor smoking ban worked somewhere else, but will it also work in my region/country?).

Secondly, once the 'right evidence' has been collected to substantiate and identify the issue at stake (fracking may cause environmental damage), you still have to translate that research into policy and effective action (how to mitigate that damage). Hence the need to show that your proposed solution will indeed prove effective in tackling the problem (to enable fracking only when it does not lead to water pollution). Yet many actions can do both good and harm, and the potential for both may be unevenly distributed in the population. So it is often necessary to assess the overall balance between risks and benefits, as well as how these are distributed among different members of the population. In relation to our fracking example, while the benefits of fracking may outweigh the costs for the average citizen, it poses significant risks for those who live close to fracking sites given the significant level of contamination of both the soil and the air. A further problem is whether an intervention that is effective in a research setting will prove equally effective in a real-world context. This may involve complex mathematical and statistical modelling and, in the case of behavioural-informed intervention,[10] randomised control trials.[11]

Thirdly, given that many policy interventions involve lots of separate measures, it is often difficult to pinpoint the impact of a single one. What if tobacco taxes are the real reason that people are giving up smoking, rather than bans on lighting up indoors?

In sum, the numerous factors at stake in the underlying problem you want to tackle, the interdisciplinary character of the evidence available and the difficulty in proving the individual effectiveness of different policy options are some of the major challenges for any citizen lobbying campaign.

TIP 5 – Be Data-Driven, Even Without Data

It is not always possible to put a figure on the benefits and costs of your proposed action. As benefits tend to be more difficult to quantify than costs (because, as opposed to costs, they belong to the unknown), you might find yourself up against the wall. This should not, however, prevent you from showing decision-makers the qualitative data in your proposal: identifying who would bear the costs, who would benefit and why. This will allow policymakers and their aides to understand whether your concept is achievable. They might even do the maths themselves!

Evidence on the Precedents

Has anyone already tried to engage with your issue (or a similar one) in the past? You might be surprised by how many previous attempts have been made, perhaps in other parts of the world, at addressing your issue. But great minds think alike, right?

Looking for precedents is key for citizen lobbying, because we don't have unlimited resources. And in the process of finding out about previous initiatives, you may find out why they failed. Even if you can dig out just one prior attempt, campaign or mere analysis of your issue, it might prove a real treasure trove of information. Here are some of the questions that should drive your hunt for precedents:

- Who sponsored (and/or supported) the initiative?
- How long ago?
- What exactly was proposed?
- Why did it fail?
- Who opposed the idea and on what grounds?

For instance, I recently discovered that in Italy more than 58 bills have been lodged to regulate professional lobbying. Yet none have made it through. Getting hold of those bills might be key to understand the challenges ahead for an action aimed at promoting the regulation of professional lobbying in Italy.

During your research you might come across countries or regions that have already adopted your solution, but perhaps in a different way. This set of precedents may expand your understanding of both the issue you want to tackle and its possible solutions. Successful precedents will show what is and isn't possible within a given context. Once more, your research efforts come with a bonus: while searching for precedents, you are likely to bump into key people who have been involved in your issue. These people are probably as passionate about the issue as you are, and may be keen to help you pass or oppose similar policies or actions in your territory. And, as veteran campaigners on the issue, they might share with you the major difficulties and successes and tell you how the policy was implemented (Step 10). Often neglected, this step of any lobbying action demands a great deal of attention, as it may determine whether your work will be worth the effort. People who were involved in previous campaigns can even tell you what they would do differently and thereby save you from a few mistakes.

TIP 6 – Precedents Matter

Looking for previous attempts at solving your issue may prove a treasure trove. You enrich your data collection when it comes to defining the extent and nature of the problem, and you back up your proposed solution. You uncover individuals and organisations who have worked on the issue – or would like to do so. You learn from their successes and past mistakes. Finally, reaching out puts the plausibility of your plans to the test again.

Factsheet

All the information that you've gathered through your research must first be summed up in a background document (Activity 3). This document is generally several pages long and contains an appendix citing the many studies, figures and data that you have gathered.

The background file, being an internal document, should not be circulated beyond the core team. It must then be distilled into a single two-sided sheet for external use, called the factsheet (or 'one-pager'). This shorter document will provide a succinct summary of everything you have learned about your issue and why it supports your solution. It will be used to persuade everyone who will be meeting to discuss your issue – decision-makers, their assistants, journalists, friends or potential funders. The reader must be able to understand quickly what the issue is about and how you propose to address it.

The most important items to include in the factsheet are:

1. Title of the action (which is often replaced by the branding – Step 7)

2. A brief blurb stating the issue

3. Facts underlying the nature and extent of the issue (to be footnoted)

4. A story giving a face to your issue (include an image and/or quote) (Tip 4)

5. A brief blurb of your proposed solution

6. Facts supporting the effectiveness of your solution (to be footnoted)

7. A brief presentation of the avenue(s) that you intend to follow and related tactics (Step 4) (Tip 5)

8. A list of groups and organisations who support your action (Step 5)

9. The name and contact information of one of your core group members whose job it is to interact with the public (generally she/he is the communications officer)

10. The campaign website address

The quality and depth of your research will determine how seriously decision-makers, the media and the public will take you. The process of gathering and sometimes producing this information is key to the success of your citizen lobbying action. It will inform virtually all the subsequent steps, and be constantly updated.

TIP 7 – Appearance Matters: Make the Factsheet Slick!

The factsheet must speak for your campaign. It must convey your passion about the problem and testify to the plausibility of your solution. Make sure you produce a neat, catchy and succinct document. It will need a clear heading and/or branding, a neat font in a legible size and bullet points as well as box-outs. Don't hesitate to ask a (pro bono) graphic designer to transform your Word document into an appealing two-sided sheet capable of drawing attention to your cause.

STEP 3: Map Your Lobbying Environment

Your problem does not exist in a vacuum. You need to have a grasp of the complex web of different political, economic and social dynamics that relate to your issue. To do so, before designing your lobbying plan (aimed at selling your big idea), you must draw up a map identifying the major actors who have some stake in what you want to change. In so doing you must keep in mind both the background document and the factsheet. By providing context, these documents will help you pinpoint the major actors.

The map is a working tool allowing you to identify:

- the lobbying target – the relevant policymakers
- your allies – actors you can work, build and share resources with
- your supporters – people you want on your side
- your opponents – people who disagree with you and may resist and oppose change
- the influencers – other people who exert influence on your target

List Your Stakeholders

The target of your action is your major stakeholder. This is the individual or group with the power to make the change you advocate. In today's society, it is rare to find a situation in which power is held by one individual. Generally, multiple people will exercise influence on your target, including your supporters, potential allies and opponents. 'Key influencers' or secondary targets, such as the media, celebrities and other opinion leaders, are really important too. You need to be aware of who all these people are.

Going back to our story of the Alcohol Marketing Restrictions (page 114), the potential stakeholders may be listed like this:

Potential stakeholders
- Health community: health organisations and grassroots health activists
- National politics: the government, ministers, MPs, devolved nations' representatives and assemblies/national parliaments, government departments
- Local politicians: local mayor, councillors, leader of the council and the unelected council executive
- Communities: community leaders, faith leaders, local charities and community groups, school governors, the local Police and Crime Commissioner and police officials
- Prominent influencers: celebrities and high-profile individuals, academics, national charities and think tanks

- Businesses: local businesses and employers, national and multinational corporations

This list includes those who benefit from the status quo, those who would benefit from the change and groups that might be affected – even if we don't yet know how each group would benefit or lose out.

Identifying whom to lobby is just as important as deciding the issue itself. You need to know everyone who has the power to influence your cause and help make a change. But how do you decide whom to talk to? The decision generally depends on your overall lobbying and communication plans. Should it be the elected politicians, the career civil servants or the political appointees who are working the issue and may have sway?

You should gather information about their personal background and their role in relation to the issue – who is responsible for drafting a policy proposal? Who manages the team promoting an initiative? If you target an elected official, you should find a way to involve at least one of her constituents. Their involvement means she is more likely to listen to your plea.

ACTIVITY 5 – Identify Lobbying Target(s)

List all the major stakeholders in relation to your battle. In particular, list the people who have the power to make the change you want to see and the individuals/groups who can influence them.

TIP 8 – Stakeholder Profiling

When identifying stakeholders, it can be useful to profile each one. You may want to model the profile on the following criteria:

- mission (social justice, women's rights, etc.);

- funding (industry funded, foundation, member fees, etc.);

- demographics (age, race, gender, ethnicity, religion, education);

- stance (how do they perceive the issue? Are they passive or proactive?);

- geography (local, national, international; urban or rural);

- media habits (list the media most used by that organisation).

This profiling will be very useful when you come to devise the lobbying plan (Step 4), build a coalition (Step 5) and create the communication plan (Step 7).

Map Your Stakeholders, Allies and Opponents

Within each of these categories of people – decision-makers, supporters and opponents – there might be great diversity. In my alcohol marketing action, both the decision-makers and public health advocates support change. But they do it with varying intensity and, as a result, they carry different weight in the campaign. So you need to unpack and visualise their exact position on the issue – which you can do by mapping them on a power matrix. This graph allows you to visualise how power is distributed and thus will help you decide on whom to focus your energy.

Draw a horizontal and a vertical axis on a large sheet of paper. Map the list of stakeholders you have identified as follows:

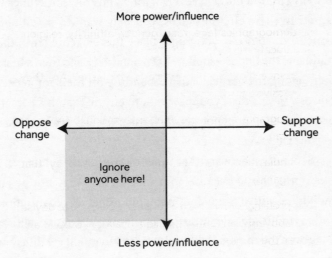

© Alberto Alemanno

The vertical axis indicates individuals' or groups' level of influence on your path to achieving your campaign goal, from most influential (top) to least influential (bottom). The horizontal axis indicates whether they are likely to oppose (left) or support (right) your action. This map captures each stakeholder's level of support and level of influence in the context of your campaign.

Your lobbying target will generally stand in the upper boxes of this matrix, but, depending on their stance towards your proposed change, they might be on the left quadrant (oppose) or the right (support). Your supporters and allies stand on the right side of the matrix, and will be in the upper or lower quadrant depending on their influence.

There are three important caveats. Firstly, while it is usually easy to find out what each actor stands for, sometimes it is not. In these circumstances, you may want to map them as neutral. To do so, you might place that stakeholder in the middle of the oppose-support horizontal axis, and then situate them along the vertical axis (depending on their influence/power). In this case, you may want to ensure that this person or organisation does not step forward and lean left in response to your campaign.

Secondly, be aware that none of your stakeholders is a monolith. This is because your interlocutor may not be an individual with a singular opinion but rather an organisation with a multitude of contrasting opinions. As a result, within any government (your lobbying target) you might get different reactions, some friendlier than others. The same applies to an NPO that might agree to team up with you. To remedy this risk of internal fragmentation within a given interlocutor, you may want to understand not only the formal organisation but also the informal one.[12] This is the network of relationships that the internal actors form across functions and divisions to accomplish tasks quickly or to slow them down.

Thirdly, opponents are not a given. Indeed, you should not always assume that your action will face major opposition.

Sometimes your issue may attract general empathy. Who doesn't want to help disabled people, or take action against paedophiles? Yet you still have to map all the stakeholders to identify those you will need to prompt to act.

ACTIVITY 6 – Draw a Power Map

Copy the power map onto a piece of paper. Place all the actors you have previously listed onto the map: lobbying target(s), supporters (and potential allies), opponents, influencers.

Once you have filled in your power map, double check it to make sure that everybody appears in it, including those actors whom you expect to oppose you. You might find that you have more supporters than you initially thought. Make sure you include organisations that have worked on the issue in the past, both for and against. Why reinvent the wheel?

Now that you have the completed map, you should focus on the actors in (or close to) the middle. What you want to do first is find out whether, and if so how, you could move those who share your point of view (or at least do not oppose you) closer to your side so as to strengthen the support and enthusiasm of indifferent and mildly pro actors. Second, you want to identify those who oppose your stance but might be keen on allying themselves with you if you address their concerns. Identify these actors, study their positions on the issue and try to meet them – because their movement to the left or right may have a big impact on your efforts, depending on how influential they are.

This mapping exercise will help you prepare the ground for coalition-building. It will also enable you to anticipate some of the arguments the various groups may make in relation to your action. The results of this forecasting can be captured by another positional map.

TIP 9 – Make a Positional Map with Movable Text Boxes

Once the major stakeholders are positioned on the power matrix, you need to consider their relationships with other entities affected by the issue. Create clusters of actors who have taken up similar positions, even if their influence or activity differs. As their positioning might change, especially if you previously classified them as neutral, you can use a Post-it note to represent each actor, ranking them according to their level of support for your cause. The result is a spectrum of stakeholders.

STEP 4: Lobbying Plan

By now, you should have identified the problem (Step 1) and its solution (Step 2), and have backed them both up with evidence. You should also have identified all the individuals and groups who hold power and those who are liable to support or oppose your action, drawing from this your key targets, allies and opponents (Step 3). You now need to draw up the best possible strategy to persuade decision-makers to adopt your solution, devising a comprehensive citizen lobbying plan. This is the 'grand strategy' that will bring about change on your issue and which will probably require a communication plan (Step 7).

The lobbying plan means strategically identifying the avenue(s) you intend to follow (e.g. legislative, administrative, judicial, political, public campaigning) and the tools you intend to use (e.g. a legislative proposal, complaint, legal action, letter, meeting, online petition).

You can visualise which tools to use for which avenues as shown in the diagram on the next page.

Inside or Outside Lobbying?

The first major strategic choice you face is whether to keep a low profile by *not* engaging with the public (inside lobbying) or to go public (outside lobbying). If you engage in 'inside lobbying', you stick to the halls of parliament and direct your action exclusively towards political parties and government. If you choose 'outside lobbying' you'll engage with the general public and media.[13]

There may be strategic reasons why you want to adopt a reserved approach at first, before going on to voice your concerns to the wider public. In some circumstances, you might gain more by acting behind closed doors than by publicly campaigning. While we might be tempted to go for outside lobbying *because* decision-makers might see it as a threat and thus capitulate to us, outside lobbying isn't always necessary. Indeed, arranging a face-to-face meeting

ISSUE

(e.g. to reduce smoking, to ban fracking, to fight LGBT discrimination)

ACTION

(e.g. to ban indoor smoking, to restrict fracking, to promote civil rights legislation)

AVENUE

| Campaign | Legislative | Administrative | Judicial | Political |

TOOLS

| Informal petition
Self-publication
Stickers
Gadgets | Petition
Legislative proposal
Public consultation | FOIA
Complaint review
Ombudsman | Legal challenge | Meeting
Letter
Op-Ed |

©Alberto Alemanno

with a decision-maker to share an idea with them or to propose an amendment to an existing text might turn out to be more effective than running a full-blown campaign. In our Alcohol Marketing Restrictions project, we first asked for a meeting with the competent policymaker (the EU Health Commissioner) and, as he refused to meet us, we had no choice but to go for outside lobbying.

Never forget that your goal is to induce change – by promoting or opposing an initiative – rather than to get people together just for the sake of it. Too often activists get carried away and transform their actions into ends in themselves – an exercise of voice, without real influence. That's why I always advise anyone who wants to start a citizen lobbying action such as a petition – whether official or unofficial (the latter might be hosted on a commercial online platform, such as Avaaz) – or a march or protest to meet relevant decision-makers beforehand. I advise you to do this not because I believe you should ask their permission before you act, but because giving prior notice of a public campaign can act as a powerful nudge to decision-makers. Even if they aren't in a position to immediately act on your call, they will appreciate that you alerted them to what you were planning. The mere prospect of a formal administrative complaint or an online petition may deter decision-makers from (or push them towards) action. In other words, as a result of your heads up, the ball will be in their – not your – court.

Your choice of lobbying approach (inside vs outside) shapes the avenues and tools of action you will adopt. An inside strategy will involve internal tactics such as:

- proposing new policy initiatives,
- suggesting amendments to pending legislation, and
- meeting face-to-face with policymakers.

An outside strategy typically calls for external tactics such as:

- petitions,
- digital campaigning, and
- other forms of outreach.

Inside and outside lobbying approaches are not mutually exclusive, and the avenues each uses can (and must) be combined. You can start 'inside' by asking for a meeting. If that's refused, you may want to go 'outside' by launching a petition. In any event, be aware that face-to-face meetings and direct involvement with the policy process are inescapable. They represent the core business of any lobbying effort.

Finally, your overall lobbying strategy will determine the choice (and combination) of avenue(s) of action you pick, and the tools you use. In turn, this determines virtually all your next steps, from branding to coalition building. These are important choices, so make sure the strategy and tactics you choose match what you and your team can comfortably do.

The Avenues

Various avenues are open to you as a citizen to voice your concern in the public sector – be it with your elected representatives or with civil servants. In this section, we are going to look at the major courses of action that may be open to you.

As this is the most technical step you are going to undertake, this guide introduces you to the major features, core concepts, and dos and don'ts of each avenue, as well as providing a few signposts for those wishing to find out more.

The avenues you can choose include:

- 'political' by sending a letter to your elected representative(s);

- 'legislative' to bring about policy change;

- 'administrative' to complain against your public administration;

- 'judicial' by going to court; and

- 'campaign' to bring public awareness to your issue and put pressure on decision-makers to take up a certain course of action.

Campaigning today represents both an independent avenue of action and a set of online and offline tools that can amplify and bolster the other avenues. For instance, GetUp! and its partner organisations successfully targeted the Australian government's decision to deport more than 200 asylum seekers. They relied exclusively on an online petition and street protests. OneSingleTariff, on the other hand, launched a media campaign to attract signatures in support of the European Citizens' Initiative – a transnational petition system – to put an end to international roaming charges across European countries.

The nature of these courses of action varies considerably, and each one calls for different skills. But what they all require is a basic understanding of how the public sector is organised and how it functions. You then need a grasp of the different tools that can be harnessed to influence decision-makers – while at the same time respecting legal constraints and procedures.

While most of the avenues open to you are formalised, and as such limit your scope of action, such as the legislative (e.g. a legislative proposal), administrative (e.g. an administrative complaint) and the judicial (e.g. a legal action), some are not. When you launch a media campaign, register a petition or simply ask for a meeting with your lobbying target, your scope for action is practically limitless. Nonetheless, be aware that the choice of avenue is often pre-determined by the state of the debate surrounding your issue – or by the policy process itself. If a legislative proposal has been put forward and you want to oppose it, your action will inevitably engage at the legislative level (e.g. by proposing amendments). This does not, however, stop you from using alternative avenues, such as a media campaign or an administrative complaint, if the public authorities have failed to do their job.

Your lobbying plan is about identifying the avenues available and then strategically deciding which one(s) to prioritise.

Each avenue offers different institutional and informal tools you can use to prompt change, such as petitions, social networks and Freedom of Information Act (FOIA) requests.

The Legislative Avenue

Professional lobbying activity largely revolves around the legislative process. It is mostly about influencing the outcome of a legislative initiative or promoting a new initiative from scratch. Sometimes, it can also be about opposing initiatives or existing legislation. Although a citizen lobbyist tends to deploy a wider range of tools – and of a more unconventional kind – than a professional, she will also typically engage with formal policy processes to induce change. The key is to gain a good understanding of the constitutional arrangements governing your system[14] by asking these simple questions:

- *Which level of government is responsible for my issue?* This can be national, local and sometimes federal. Addressing this question is vital because it determines the 'right' actors to lobby.

- *How many layers of government are involved?* As some law enforcement is delegated to local authorities, it may be overruled by the central government. So even if you win at a local level, you may still lose at a national or federal one.

Once you have addressed and understood these constitutional constraints, you can identify your lobbying targets and the ways to move your issue forward.

The third question you need to ask, if you haven't yet done so, is:

- *Has the issue already been dealt with?* In other words,

should your lobbying efforts aim at changing an existing policy, or promoting a new one?

Two main scenarios are possible: either the issue has already been tackled, but you want a policy change – or no action has been taken, and you're lobbying for it to happen.

Policy Change

Generally, citizen lobbying actions focus on changing – or resisting changes to – an already existing policy. To succeed you need to convince decision-makers to change (or maintain) the law.

When the policy change has already been announced, or is ongoing, you need to make sure you understand at which stage in the process the initiative stands (Step 2). Your influence will vary depending on where it stands: the sooner you intervene in the process, the greater your influence will be. For instance, in the EU, the curve of influence looks like this:

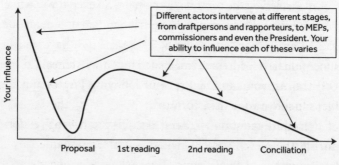

Different actors intervene at different stages, from draftpersons and rapporteurs, to MEPs, commissioners and even the President. Your ability to influence each of these varies

© Alberto Alemanno

When the policy process has already started, you have several opportunities to shape it, the most frequent of which are:

- the public consultation process, which is generally open during the preparation of the policy proposal;
- policy amendments.

Below are a few examples of how the policy process works in various countries around the world.

Public Consultations

Public consultations during policy preparation and design are organised in different ways (e.g. open vs closed) and have different objects (legislation vs executive acts). For example, while the US notice-and-comment procedure applies exclusively to proposed rules (i.e. acts of execution of previously adopted legislation), other forms of consultation, such as the EU consultative practice, apply predominantly to the legislative process.[15]

United States Notice-and-Comment

Notice-and-comment is one of the oldest and best-known stakeholder engagement mechanisms in existence. In the US, the Administrative Procedure Act (APA) originally introduced notice-and-comment in 1946 in the context of the rapid growth of federal agencies and programmes during the New Deal era, which were accompanied by a large number of regulations. This stakeholder engagement mechanism does not apply to the legislative process, but only to rulemaking – that is the process by which federal agencies implement legislation passed by Congress and signed into law by the President. As a result, only the federal agencies – not Congress – are subject to a duty to put their proposals to the attention of the public. Bills are not subject to public consultation, only rules are.

Under notice-and-comment, virtually all federal agency rulemaking is governed first and foremost by APA §553, which entails a three–step rulemaking process:

i.   The agency publishes a Notice of Proposed Rulemaking (NPRM) in the Federal Register. This NPRM contains a proposed draft of the rule, backed by a brief explanation and a request for comments.

ii.   The agency receives comments and modifies the draft rule as appropriate.

iii. The agency issues a final rule accompanied by a pre-amble in which it explains the rule and responds to comments. In APA parlance, all final rules must be supported by a 'concise general statement of their basis and purpose'.

Notice-and-comment accomplishes the first two forms of engagement: information and consultation. It informs you, the public, because in most instances, the NPRM offers the first official glimpse that the public at large gets of the agency's approach to the rule. The NPRM is immediately followed by a public comment (consultation) period of a length that is set by the agency in the NPRM itself. The third form of public engagement – participation – is absent.

EU Consultation Practice

To ensure that 'the Union's actions are coherent and transparent', the European Commission – the only body to initiate EU legislation – is mandated to 'carry out broad consultations with parties concerned'.[16]

Consultation can be carried out on any or all of the distinct elements of an impact assessment: determining the nature of the regulatory problem, identifying policy objectives and policy options, and assessing the costs and benefits of each option. Consultation is not a one-off event; it runs throughout the preparation phase of both the draft Impact Assessment (IA) and the proposal. Therefore, it requires the preparation of a consultation plan that determines:

- the objective of the consultation;

- the elements for which this is necessary – nature of the problem, policy options, etc.;

- the target group – general public or a special category of stakeholders;

- the appropriate consultation tool – consultative committees, expert groups, ad hoc meetings, online consultation, etc.; and

- the appropriate time frame.

The Commission's guidelines stipulate a minimum period for written public consultations of twelve weeks, and twenty working days' notice for meetings. While the guidelines encourage the Commission to provide feedback and take the comments received into account, they differ from the US system in that the guidelines do not require comments or Commission responses to be incorporated as such in the preamble or the text of the rule (though they do need to be reflected in the IA report). In practice, the Commission publishes a report that sums up the main findings gathered via the consultation and circulates it among stakeholders before finalising its draft IA and accompanying proposal.

New Zealand Participatory Mechanism

One of the most interesting examples of a participatory mechanism enabling stakeholder engagement in policy development exists in New Zealand. Here, after the first reading, bills are open to public comments. Any citizen is invited to make submissions on the bill, give evidence and recommend amendments to the legislator, who is expected to reprint a copy of the bill alongside a report explaining the reasons for any recommended amendment based on the evidence gathered.[17]

Policy Dialogue

Another instrument to enable citizens to engage in policy preparation is called policy dialogue. It involves people from different interest groups sitting together around a table to focus on an issue in which they have a mutual, but not necessarily common, interest. It assumes that people in different positions will have different perspectives on the same problem.

STORY – The Dutch Energy Agreement for Sustainable Growth

The Dutch Energy Agreement for Sustainable Growth was signed in 2013 between the Dutch government and 48 different stakeholders. It sought to reform the Dutch energy sector and make it more sustainable through ten major commitments by the government and its stakeholders. The aims were to reduce energy use, increase the proportion of green electricity in the mix and create more jobs. The agreement was negotiated and signed within an advisory body to the Dutch government on socioeconomic matters, which was the initiator and organiser of the agreement.

Forty-eight different organisations representing a wide variety of interests took part in the negotiations and signed the eventual agreement. These organisations varied from environmental organisations to employers' forums, labour unions and sectorial interest groups. Scientists, politicians and citizens also participated in the discussions and negotiations. A particular feature of the agreement was that some commitments were undertaken by private parties outside the public policy framework, pre-empting the need for government intervention.[18]

TIP 10 – Submit Your Observations

Consider taking part in any public consultation, or policy dialogue that affects your issue.

A consultation may give you an opportunity not only to shape the forthcoming proposal but also to meet and talk to the decision-makers. You can leverage your submission to obtain a meeting (or at least a brief exchange) about the issue you care about.

Policy Amendments

Generally, if you want to revise a bill or proposal, you need to put forward an amendment. But since this is the prerogative of decision-makers, you cannot act alone. You need to identify the key decision-makers able to amend that policy, or a new proposal, and put forward your own draft amendments. Recently, my students and I drafted an amendment to the existing EU Passengers' Rights Regulation, which provides a minimum level of protection for air passengers when a flight that they intended to travel on is delayed or cancelled, when they are denied boarding due to overbooking or when the airline is unable to accommodate them in the class for which they had paid.

Our amendment aimed to prohibit the use of 'no show' clauses in your flight ticket. This clause means that if you do not show up for the outbound flight – the first leg of your journey – you will be deemed a no-show, and all the connecting flights associated with this one, even a return flight, will be cancelled and no refund will apply. Many of us will have personal experience of a no-show clause!

When you get involved in public consultations and/or in policy amendments, you may want to tell the public about your action. Submitting a set of observations or draft amendments can give you the chance to mobilise popular support. This can be done through various forms of external communication, including petitions.

TIP 11 – Draft Your Amendment

You might not be expecting your decision-maker to welcome practical and tangible help during the legislative process. However, it is common practice to prepare and share draft amendments or even full texts with decision-makers, with the aim of making their job easier during the legislative process.

Indeed, there is nothing inherently improper about a person or entity outside the parliament or the government doing the main drafting for proposed legislation, provided two conditions are satisfied:

- the proposal must go through the normal legislative process of public consultations, debates, committee and floor votes, etc.;

- the public should know who wrote the draft amendment or proposal.

Unfortunately, as the general public does not seem to appreciate just how often this occurs, no country seems to guarantee the latter condition. So I advise you always to let the public know what you are proposing to decision-makers. It is okay to be smart, but only if you are transparent!

Policy Initiation

Sometimes no-one, neither the public official nor the government, seems interested in taking action on your issue. And as a citizen, you cannot initiate (or block) the legislative process. Generally, this is the prerogative of elected representatives and governments acting both at a local and national level. In this situation, citizen lobbying is a different ballgame. In the absence of a policy or policy proposal, your action has to start earlier. You need to start from scratch.

How? You can meet the decision-makers, pick up the phone or send a letter to share your idea for a new proposal with them. If you are in a position to do so, put forward an actual text for a legislative proposal.

That's what I did – together with my students and several colleagues – in the framework of a project with Transparency International and the Greens. We drafted the first legislative proposal aimed at protecting whistle-blowers across the European Union, engaging the legislators in our lobbying campaign as we did so. When you take this path, you essentially do the work of the decision-makers by showing them that:

i.   there is an issue;
ii. there is a solution;

iii. the solution is viable and they should embrace and support it.

There's no reason to take the credit: just put your work in the decision-makers' hands. In less than a year's time from the finalisation of our text, the policymakers – notably the EU Commission under pressure from the EU Parliament – have decided to step in and provide a minimum level of protection for whistle-blowers in Europe.[19] That means that all European member states will be expected to afford protection to whistle-blowers acting in their territories.

This story illustrates that while policymakers are typically the ones taking the legislative initiative, you have opportunities as a citizen to prompt the legislative process. A significant number of countries already give the public the opportunity to initiate policy by submitting ideas, proposals or requests to governments. Referendums, official (as opposed to commercial) petitions and popular initiatives are typical examples. Contrary to conventional wisdom, these citizen-initiated mechanisms of direct democracy are not meant to replace representative democracy, but to complement it.[20] They enable citizens and other stakeholders to put issues on the political agenda that policymakers would prefer not to discuss.[21] These types of mechanisms are available in the vast majority of countries,[22] and can be regarded as an expression of participatory decision-making in contemporary democracy. Depending on how these pre-legislative mechanisms are governed within each legal system, they involve different forms of engagement.[23]

Referendums

A referendum is a form of direct democracy which involves an electorate-wide vote on an issue of public policy. Depending on the country's legal system, referendums may be initiated by the citizens, generally through a citizens' initiative, by a legislative act or by a governmental executive order. In different countries a referendum may be used to initiate policy or, more frequently, for consultative purposes. They can therefore enter the policy process at different levels and cover very different subjects. You could call for a referendum to promote or oppose a given action. In Italy, they have been successfully used by groups who wanted to adopt laws allowing divorce and abortion in the 1970s. They are still used today.

Referendums take many forms. They may aim to change institutions (such as rules about the length of presidential terms), to adopt new policies (such as the privatisation of public utilities in Uruguay or the approval by Costa Rica of a trade agreement with the US), or to make a constitutional shift (such as the Irish referendum on the EU's Lisbon Treaty). Moreover, their legal status (mandatory vs voluntary), requirements (collection of signatures, etc.), as well as consequences (consultative or legally binding) vary considerably.

Petitions

Petitioning is a well-established form of political participation in most liberal democracies. A petition is a request to do something, most commonly addressed to a government official or public entity. Although historically it has never really been seen as anything more than a last-ditch personal effort to attract favour or attention from the highest authority, it has regained some popularity over the last decade thanks to the possibilities provided by the internet.

A petition generally consists of a document addressed to some decision-makers, signed by numerous individuals. A petition may be oral rather than written, but nowadays is most often sent online. This is called e-petitioning. However, a key distinction exists between official online petitions and those submitted through commercial online petition platforms, such as Avaaz or Change. Only the former qualify as an 'administrative avenue', since these e-petition platforms operate within the rules that apply in your country. For instance, if you fail to ensure that everyone signing the petition is a national or resident of your country, it may be rejected. Likewise, failing to collect the required number of signatures may mean the authorities have no duty to act upon, or even respond to your request. An unofficial platform, such as Avaaz, lacks these constraints. Furthermore, no number of signatures collected on unofficial platforms necessitates that decision-makers respond to you. Generally, petitioners resort to Avaaz or Change when the official petition does not work out or when they want to obtain more signatures than they could otherwise do. This, however, presupposes that the signatures collected on the commercial platforms are verified as valid by the official petition system. A petition on the wrong platform, to the wrong people, or signed by people who live outside the relevant jurisdiction, is a waste of time and effort, at least from the public authorities' perspective.

Although a petition is only as meaningful as its response, it allows blocks of public interest to form, harnessing power in ways that may lead to a legislative or administrative response. Whether you want to promote a new policy, to change a law or a behaviour, to get a decision made, or simply to raise awareness of an issue, petitions can be a relatively easy and inexpensive way to get the word out.

Indeed, they have a long history of bringing about significant change. In the US, a petition demanding an end to slavery gathered 130,000 signatures and nudged Congress towards taking action. The digital revolution has transformed petitioning as an active instrument. In 2012, an informal Avaaz petition attracted 2.8m supporters and led MEPs to vote down the Anti-Counterfeiting Trade Agreement (ACTA). This treaty would have allegedly limited fundamental rights, including freedom of expression and internet privacy protections. (See page 209 for the full story.)

How to Do It

If you want to start a petition, all you have to do is to learn whether there are rules governing its registration (e.g. formal requirements, such as policy areas) and collection of signatures (number of signatures, residence requirements, etc.) in your country. In other words, stick to the rules set out by the governmental authority. For example:

- How many signatures will you need?

- Must all signatures be certified?

- How should people's names be included (printed, signed, or both?)

- Should addresses be included?

- What other information must be included by the signatory, or by the submitter?

- Are there limitations you must stick to, or quotas you must meet (for example, signatures per district or region)?

- When must the petitions be returned by, and to whom?

Once you know the rules of the game, you need to allow users to enter their names and other required information – and perhaps to opt in to hear more about your progress – and then store and report on this data. It can also be useful to display publicly the list of people who have signed (if signatories have agreed to share this data).

Now that you're aware of the relevant rules, you need to design your petition:

- prepare a short and attention-grabbing headline;

- tell people in the first two sentences why they should sign;

- explain why you are passionate about the issue;

- make an emotional connection with the reader.

Starting an official petition is easier and more effective than ever before. Since 2000, a number of countries have introduced electronic petition systems (e-petitions). By now, e-petitions have moved beyond the experimental stage and both citizens and governments are familiar with them.

The EU Petition System

In the EU, citizens and residents of a member state enjoy the right to address a petition to the European Parliament. If you are lucky, you may be invited to attend a hearing of the petition committee. Indeed, any individual 'has the right to address a petition to the European Parliament if it concerns a matter that comes within the European Union's field of activity and affects them directly'.[24]

You can also submit an EU petition in association with others, as an organisation or association (as long as it has its headquarters in the EU). Your petition may take the form of a complaint, a request, an observation on the application of EU law or an appeal to the European Parliament to adopt a position on a specific matter. It may relate to issues of public or private interest. Regardless, your petition must relate to a topic which falls within the EU's fields of activity and which affects you directly.

You can submit it electronically or in 'paper' form, with no standard format to be followed. Your petition may include attachments, including copies of any supporting documents you may have. You can start your own petition or support other people's. Such petitions give the European Parliament the opportunity to draw attention to any infringement of a European citizen's rights by a member state, local authorities or another institution. Your petition allows Parliament, through its Petitions Committee, to conduct an ongoing reality check on the way in which European legislation is implemented, and to measure the extent to which European institutions are responding to your concerns. The objective of the Petitions Committee is to provide a response to all petitions and, when possible, to provide a non-judicial remedy to legitimate concerns.[25]

In 2014 the European Parliament received 2,714 petitions, of which about 60 per cent were admissible and acted upon. This is about a thousand more than were received five years earlier and confirms a growing public interest in the petition system, which has been further facilitated by the electronic platform, social media and the live-streaming of parliamentary sessions. Moreover, in certain cases, the Petitions Committee may refer a petition to other European Parliament committees for information or further action, thus acting as a catalyst to bring parties together to respond to citizens' concerns. As a result, a committee might take a petition into account in its legislative activities, which essentially consists of examining the European Commission's proposals for adoption, or persuading the EU Commission to initiate an infringement proceeding against the relevant EU country. The petition system therefore offers an indirect way for you to go down the legislative avenue by presenting a draft amendment, or down the judicial avenue, by making arguments that may lead the EU Commission to take your country to court.

The US Petition System

The White House has set up a platform for citizen petitions called We the People. US citizens may initiate a petition by submitting a short abstract. If it gathers more than 25,000 signatures in 30 days, the White House identifies an expert in the government to respond to the petition. The responses are then published on the White House website.

The UK Petition System

Similarly, UK residents can petition the government and the parliament on a dedicated platform.[26] Petitions that reach 10,000 signatures get a response from the government. At 100,000 signatures, they are considered for debate in Parliament. So far, out of the 21,000 petitions that have been started on the platform, 276 petitions have drawn a response from the government, with 30 having been debated in the House of Commons. The day after the Brexit vote – the referendum in which the UK voted to leave the European Union – a petition calling for a second referendum was so popular that the website crashed for several hours.

The Westminster Parliament has also ensured that petitioners can contact people who have supported them, to inform them of the response in a very efficient way. This site superseded the Number 10 web portal, over which Parliament had no authority. A Hansard Society report on the petitions process paved the way for this significant new development.

The Irish Petition System

The Republic of Ireland established the Oireachtas Committee on Investigations, Oversight and Petitions in 2011, implementing a manifesto commitment of the main coalition parties. It has since been pivotal in enabling greater citizen

involvement in political affairs. The petitions process connects, in this context, the citizen to a parliament, which, in
turn, has a duty and a responsibility to respond and provide
answers and explanations – even remedies – to the petitioner.

The Canadian Petition System

In Canada, the House of Commons now hosts an e-petitions
platform on its website. For an e-petition to be posted to the
website for signing, the main petitioner has to find five signatories. They also have to find an MP who agrees to sponsor it
in the House. Only once this has happened will the petition
appear online (assuming everything else about it is in order).
An e-petition remains open for signatures for 120 days. To
receive final certification and be presented in the House of
Commons, an e-petition must receive a minimum of 500 valid
signatures during this period. If it fails to gather the minimum number of valid signatures, it proceeds no further, but
remains visible online.

To sum up, when used and managed effectively, a petitions
process can enhance the parliamentary process and strengthen
its representative function.

For an overview of unofficial online petition platforms,
see the Public Campaigning avenue (page 202).

Initiatives

Another instrument that can be used to get policymaking
started is the 'initiative', sometimes called an 'agenda initiative'.

Only a few countries provide for citizens' initiatives.

Australia and New Zealand do by enabling citizens who collect a minimum of 10 per cent of signatures in support of their petition to compel governments to hold a referendum on that issue. Supporters of a particular citizens' initiative have one year in which to collect their signatures. Note that the results of the citizens' initiated referendums are 'indicative' only: they are not binding on Parliament or government.

The EU has recently established its own mechanism: the European Citizens' Initiative (ECI). The ECI is the first transnational instrument of participatory democracy in the world. It allows 1 million citizens from at least seven EU Member States to invite the European Commission 'to submit a proposal on matters where citizens consider that a legal act of the Union is required for the purpose of implementing the Treaties'. There are several steps before an ECI can be submitted to the Commission. To launch an initiative, a citizens' committee has to be set up. The committee must be composed of at least seven EU citizens, who must live in at least seven different EU countries. Before it starts collecting signatures, this committee has to register its proposal on the Commission's website. Then, upon the Commission's validation of the initiative (admissibility review), the initiators have to collect 1 million signatures from across the EU – face-to-face or online. The time limit is a year from the date of registration. On top of this, organisers need to have a minimum number of signatories from at least seven EU countries.

Once these steps are completed, the European Commission meets with the organisers so they can explain the initiative in detail. Within three months, the Commission sets out its legal and political conclusions, the action it intends to take and its reasons for acting (or not). Then the organisers are given the opportunity to present their initiative at a public hearing in the European Parliament. Unfortunately, due to the number of constraints (both legal and practical), only a few initiatives have successfully completed the ECI process from initial registration to Commission acceptance and reply. Out of 50 plus registered ECIs, only three have collected the million signatures required and only one, the Right2Water campaign, led the EU to act. More than 40 per cent of initiatives were rejected by the EU, as they fell outside of its competences to act. What renders the ECI a particularly interesting instrument is its origin. It was put on the EU political agenda by a group of citizen lobbyists led by Carsten Berg. They successfully advocated for its recognition within the Treaty, establishing a Constitution for Europe prepared by the Convention on the Future of Europe and established by the EU Member States in 2001. Despite the decision of EU leaders to stop the negotiation of this treaty, which would have formally added a constitutional value to the EU, it was decided to include the ECI into the subsequent revision of the EU Treaties.

STORY – Stop TTIP

In 2014–15, 3.5 million European citizens signed an ECI – launched by Stop TTIP, an alliance of over 500 organisations – to prevent the Transatlantic Trade and Investment Partnership (TTIP) between the EU and the USA from being implemented. Thought to be the largest petition ever, it was rejected by the European Commission on legal grounds, after which the organisation restyled itself as a 'self-organised ECI'. The petition continues to gather signatures, and a lawsuit is currently underway to try to overturn the Commission's decision on the official petition.

STORY – Right2Water

The Right2Water citizens' initiative became the first ever successful ECI in 2014, after gathering 1.6 million signatures from citizens of 25 different member states. Launched in Ireland, Right2Water's credo is that access to water is a fundamental human right, and it campaigns to keep water services free from privatisation. The initiative called on the European Commission to propose legislation implementing the human right to water and sanitation as recognised by the UN, and promoted the provision of water and sanitation as essential public services. The EU legislation would require governments to provide all citizens with clean, sufficient drinking water and sanitation. Thanks to this campaign, the EU decided that public procurement rules do not apply when local authorities decide to provide the services themselves.

In the United States, direct democracy is only found at the state and local level. Twenty-four states have one or two mechanisms which allow citizens themselves to vote initiatives into law. The most powerful type is the direct initiative found in states like California and Nebraska. As with all initiatives, direct initiatives are citizen-designed legislative proposals, which other citizens can support by signing petitions. What makes the direct initiative such a powerful tool for citizenry is that after collecting the required number of signatures, the proposal goes directly before all the registered voters of the state for a vote of approval and enactment.

The slightly weaker *indirect* initiative works in the same way, except that after signature collection the state legislature must approve the proposal before citizens may vote on it. Some states like Massachusetts and Ohio even allow further signature collection to override this legislative veto. Sometimes, American courts exercise judicial review of ballot initiatives and referendums, as with the cases of *Hollingsworth v. Perry* where the decision was eventually appealed to the Supreme Court. In that case, citizens successfully filed a suit against a ballot initiative banning gay marriage. The case raised questions over whether courts should have the power to review direct democracy campaigns – a debate that also exists at national levels within the EU.

STORY – The California Taxpayers' Revolt

In the 1970s, California resident Howard Jarvis ignited a movement which came to be known as the 'taxpayers' revolt'. Angry with the high tax rate on real estate, he set up a campaign which eventually led to a state-wide referendum on the subject. The vote passed with a

near two-thirds majority, and the tax rate was subse-
quently slashed by 57 per cent with the introduction of
Proposition 13 to the Constitution of California. The
event, which triggered a similar vote and amendment in
the state of Massachusetts just two years later, is a land-
mark moment in US history.

So citizens' initiatives are not so much about direct democracy as about the power of numbers to influence rather than
compel decision-makers to do what is apparently desired by
the majority of voters.

eParticipation

A relatively new and still experimental way of getting stakeholders involved in policy and agenda-setting is through the
use of information and communication technologies (ICT).[27]
Various recent initiatives have attempted to bring citizens
and politicians together to develop public policy. The EU's
Demos@Work programme, for instance, seeks to facilitate
discussions between civil society and elected representatives
in Europe on the harmful effects of smoking. The initiative
currently has two pilots ongoing in Catalonia and Lithuania.
Another example is the EU's eCommittee project, which
seeks to gather suggestions and questions from citizens in ten
Member States and deliver them – through web conferences
– to MEPs who are working on environmental protection and
climate change. Both of these examples are part of the larger
EU eParticipation initiative.

The Administrative Avenue

Not all the policy changes or actions that you lobby for (or resist) will require a change in legislation. As a general rule, if what you want can be obtained from ministries, departments, agencies or other parts of government, you can follow the 'administrative' avenue. This is the route to take if you want existing policies to be implemented better (e.g. your LGBT law is on the statute book, but no one is acting on it). Similarly, if you're complaining about how your elected representatives, their offices and the whole administrative machine treat you (e.g. they don't respond to your requests), you should follow this avenue. Sometimes you want a given office to take a decision, such as launching an investigation into a company that is mistreating its employees or breaching environmental standards. Other times you need to force an office to disclose a document to the public (e.g. the expenses of your elected representatives).

The administrative avenue does not generally involve elected representatives, but rather focuses on civil servants (often called bureaucrats), who may be politically appointed or career-based. In some cases, you may want to challenge (or threaten to challenge) their decisions before the courts, thereby pursuing the 'judicial' avenue.

Virtually all countries recognise that their governmental bodies must act within the law (and the competences conferred upon them), and as a result they are accountable for how they treat their citizens.

The administrative avenue, similar to legislative lobbying, is limited by pre-determined procedures. These establish formal mechanisms ranging from simple requests (e.g. for access to public documents) to review and complaint procedures (e.g. a complaint to the ombudsman).

It is vital to learn about the various procedures that enable you to hold your administration accountable. While they differ from country to country, there are two privileged administrative tools that any citizen lobbyist must know about.

FOIA Requests

Historically, secrecy in politics was seen as inevitable. Yet secrecy has rapidly evolved into one of the most important citizen battles of our time. Efforts to force the authorities to abandon it led to the enactment of transparency and freedom of information laws – also called open records, sunshine laws or, most frequently, FOIAs (which take their name from various Freedom of Information Acts).[28] Over 95 countries around the world have some form of freedom of information legislation, with two-thirds of these introduced since the year 2000.[29] Quite suddenly, 5 billion people have, at least on paper, gained the legal right to access government information.

As a result, FOIA has emerged as one of the most powerful tools for a citizen lobbyist. It empowers each of us to access information from a public authority in order to ensure transparency and hold decision-makers accountable. FOIA embodies the bottom-up, do-it-yourself approach of citizen lobbying. As stated by the US Supreme Court:

The basic purpose of FOIA is to ensure an informed citizenry, vital to the functioning of a democratic society,

needed to check against corruption and to hold the governors accountable to the governed.[30]

Although each country has its own FOIA regulations and
practices (and often each agency has its own rules), they share
some common features.

FOIAs let you access information held by public authorities in two ways:

- public authorities are obliged to publish certain information about their activities (proactive transparency);

- members of the public are entitled to request information
  from public authorities (reactive transparency).

In other words, either the information is provided to us, or
we have to ask for it ourselves.

The idea behind FOIA is that people have a right to
know about what public authorities do, unless there is good
reason for them not to. Disclosure of information is the
default.

Moreover, FOIAs tend to be purpose- and applicant-blind.
This means that:

- you have the right to access official information, regardless of who you are and where you come from;

- you don't need to provide a reason for wanting the information. On the contrary, public authorities must justify
  refusing to give it to you;

- all requests are treated equally, except in a few instances relating to vexatious requests and personal data. In other words, the beauty of FOIA advocacy is that it makes no difference who you are or why you want the information – whether you are a citizen, politician, journalist, local resident, civil servant or researcher;

- any information you obtain under FOIA should be treated as if it were being released to the world at large;

- public authorities can voluntarily disclose information to certain people, outside of FOIA requests.

FOIAs allow you to gain access to any recorded information held by public authorities, such as data, printed documents, electronic files, letters, emails and photographs. Access is not limited to official documents and it therefore covers drafts, emails, notes, recordings of telephone conversations, other audio and videos as well as CCTV recordings.

They establish a 'right-to-know' legal process through which requests can be obtained freely or at minimal cost, with some exceptions.

The major advantage of FOIA advocacy is that you do not need to have legal training or use special forms to file your requests. All you need is a letter (usually an email), and in some countries you can even file your request online. Several independent platforms make it easy for you to prepare, file and track a request. Access Info Europe, a Madrid-based NGO promoting transparency in government, had the brilliant idea of setting up an open platform – AskTheEU.org

– that can be used by anyone when filing an FOIA request. Because it is public, once someone files a request anyone can track its progress and eventually gain access to the requested information. And since everyone gets to see the correspondence, people don't need to ask the same question again. A similar platform, called WhatDoTheyKnow.com, exists in the UK. In Australia, there is RighttoKnow.org.au and in New Zealand, fyi.org.nz. In the United States, a new FOIA Hub was built by the Department of Justice, but the privately run FOIA Machine is more commonly used. Despite its initial ambition, the FOIA machine does not yet allow you to file and track requests to governmental and public agencies worldwide.

A vast proportion of my own citizen lobbying campaigns started life as FOIA requests. We regularly file them both at a national and EU level. Sometimes, we do both at the same time in order to maximise our chances of success. Most of our track record is publicly available on AsktheEU.org to the benefit of anyone interested in obtaining the same document from public authorities.

STORY – Faceless Judges

Considering that some countries hold televised hearings when selecting justices for their supreme courts, there is an astonishing lack of transparency around the selection of candidates for the Courts of Justice of the European Union ('CJEU'). Every time a judge is to be appointed to the CJEU, a special panel comprised

of former judges issues an opinion on the suitabil-
ity of the candidate. This opinion is not released to
the public and is only communicated to the member
states. In 2014, my students and I used the EU FOIA
to try to get hold of these opinions. We were, however,
rebuffed by the Council of the EU (which holds the opinions). In 2015, working with Madrid-based Access Info
Europe, we drafted a complaint to the EU ombudsman.
Simultaneously, we requested access to the same panel
opinions at the national level, via member state access
to document regimes (in Poland, Austria, Germany and
the Netherlands).

The EU ombudsman told parliament in a statement
that transparency requires the EU to 'be accountable to
the citizens that it serves'.

'Access to information about how the EU and its institutions work is vital for the citizens to trust the EU, and
the EU needs the trust of its citizens especially at times
when it faces both internal and external challenges,' she
stated.

Pressure from the ombudsman forced the Council
of the EU and the special panel (which draft and hold the
secret opinions on the candidates to the court) to engage
in a careful review of their internal procedures. Finally, in
May 2016, the Council released redacted versions of the
opinions to us. Not satisfied with the level of information
provided, we continue to work alongside Access Info
Europe for greater transparency in judicial appointment.
A new FOIA request for access to the judicial opinions
has been filed, and a new complaint (and potentially litigation) is currently underway.

STORY – Wages Not Wine

After filing a Freedom of Information request, students at the University of Cambridge discovered that 123 members of the staff of King's College were being paid below the 'Living Wage' (the minimum wage deemed necessary to live comfortably in Britain, according to the Living Wage Foundation). Considering King's College spent £338,559 on wine in one year (with much of it gifted free to Fellows), students decided the college could afford to pay its staff better and campaigned to raise the college wage bill.

The students created a Facebook event, inviting others to come and protest with them outside the college. With student newspapers on their side, the story also received coverage in the national press (the *Guardian* and the *Independent*), putting considerable pressure on the college and University more broadly.

In February 2014, the King's College council voted to increase pay rates to match the Living Wage in their 2014/15 budget. In a further coup, in July 2014 the *Telegraph* reported that '[a]ll members of staff directly employed by the University of Cambridge will be paid the living wage from the beginning of August, in a victory for student campaigners.'

Administrative Complaints and Ombudsman Review

Governments typically provide an administrative complaint procedure, which grants individuals the opportunity to request a review of public authorities' actions. Anyone can file a complaint and ask public authorities to take appropriate action when there is evidence that an error has occurred, or that action should have been taken in their case.

Administrative review procedures play an essential role in preventing the state from gaining absolute power without constraints, accountability or controls.

As a citizen lobbyist, it is important to know which procedures are open to you because they may prove to be an effective and low-cost tool.

Among the various procedures, the institution of the ombudsman deserves closer scrutiny. Ombudsmen were first created in Sweden more than 200 years ago, and are intended to protect the individual where there is a substantial imbalance of power – generally between public authorities and citizens. Since then, ombudsmen have been appointed – sometimes under a different name – in many parts of the world.

The ombudsman is an open and independent public official with far-reaching powers of investigation. Her job is to act as a buffer between the individual citizen and public authorities and to stand up for citizens' right to good administration and governance.

She is essentially a 'citizens' defender', who handles their complaints. The Spanish translation, *Defensor del Pueblo* – 'defender of the people' – speaks for itself.

Government must respect and promote the fundamental rights of its people, be free from corruption and committed to preventing, in the words of the United Kingdom's parliamentary ombudsman, 'maladministration, leading to injustice'.

Ombudsmen go about this mission in a different way from any other complaint-handling institution. They therefore act as an important mechanism in the improvement of public administration. Although their job description varies, it generally has some common features:

- The ombudsman uses swift, inexpensive and informal procedures and is easily accessible. As such, she may offer a practical alternative to the 'judicial' avenue.

- She is independent so as to guarantee impartiality. Her findings and decisions are based on examination and analysis of the facts and law.

- She has the power to maintain the confidentiality of complainants where needed.

- She achieves redress for the individual, but where they identify systemic failings, she has the power to recommend changes in the work of public authorities, both individually and collectively.

- She can generally undertake a single investigation into multiple complaints about the same topic, thus avoiding duplication and excessive costs.

Her main weapons to secure action are reasoned persuasion and publicity. Generally, she can urge public authorities to act, but can also use the naming-and-shaming approach. In short, the ombudsman is a person of prestige and influence who operates with objectivity, competence, efficiency and fairness.

Ombudsman institutions play an essential role in

guaranteeing the right to access justice and fulfilling the promise of a transparent and accountable democracy.

STORY – Roma Rights and the EU Ombudsman

The Roma are one of Europe's oldest and largest ethnic minorities, and also one of the most persecuted. Between 10 and 12 million Roma people are thought to live in Europe, with settlements in each member state. In the past, they were associated with a travelling lifestyle, but this is no longer the case for most Roma. Nonetheless they struggle to access the same quality of healthcare, education, jobs and housing that other Europeans enjoy. A United Nations Human Development report about Roma in Bulgaria, the Czech Republic, Hungary, Romania and Slovakia found that 'by such measures as literacy, infant mortality and basic nutrition, most of these countries' 4 to 5 million Roma endure conditions closer to sub-Saharan Africa than Europe'.

In Italy, the Roma have endured years of discrimination. Nils Muižnieks, the Commissioner of Human Rights for the Council of Europe, wrote an open letter in 2015 which noted that Italian authorities continued to forcibly evict Roma from their homes, and compel them to live in segregated camps.

In 2012, the EU Commission launched a pilot programme investigating the discriminatory housing practices in Italy. At the time, it seemed like the first step towards a rapid improvement in the way Roma were treated in Italy. However, the public still have no idea what is happening in those discussions between the

Commission and Italy. If the Commission decides that Italy's violations of EU law warrant formal legal sanction, they can issue a letter of formal notice, which would initiate an infringement proceeding against Italy. However, since the entire process is shrouded in secrecy there is no indication of whether they have done so.

Amnesty International tried to shed light on the proceedings by requesting documentation of the discussions between Italy and the Commission under EU FOIA (Regulation 1049/2001). Normally, in order for an EU body to deny access to a document under FOIA, they need to explain how each document concerns an area of vital EU interest, and how disclosing the document to the public would harm that interest. However, the Court of Justice of the European Union has ruled that when the Commission is engaged in an infringement process, it can be presumed that the document will harm EU interests. This gives the Commission the option to deny transparency, without giving any explanation at all. In the event, it did exactly that, throwing up an impregnable wall of secrecy. As a result, neither civil society nor the Roma themselves can know for sure what is being discussed by Italy and the Commission.

The Commission's position is that secrecy is needed to preserve the negotiations. Yet the infringement process can go on for years.

In light of this, my students and I teamed up with Amnesty International and prepared:

a. a lobbying plan analysing the case law of the CJEU and proposing several strategies that Amnesty European Institutions Office (EIO) could adopt to pursue the quest for transparency;

b. a complaint to the ombudsman alleging maladmin-
    istration on the part of the Commission in refusing
    access to documents to Amnesty EIO.

The complaint to the ombudsman urged the Commission
to review its documents individually. If a document genuinely cannot be released because it would put the
negotiations at risk, and thus damage Roma rights, the
Commission should say so. What is inappropriate is
for it to say nothing, leaving millions of Roma unsure of
whether the EU is going to protect their rights.

As a result of our complaint, the EU ombudsman
opened an investigation.

The Judicial Avenue

Courts enjoy the power to review the way in which a given
policy – or administrative decision – was made, and, to a
certain extent, to review its merits. Should you fail in your
efforts to oppose or change a given policy or decision, you
can challenge it in the courts. Although the judicial avenue
belongs to the broad citizen lobbying toolbox, litigation is not
about lobbying in its purest sense. It is more about forcing
than influencing a change via the legal system.

Litigation is generally considered a remedy of last resort,
to be handled with care. Like the administrative avenue, it
imposes time limits (beyond them your action is no longer
valid) and requires specified forms. It does, however, demand
significantly more resources and skills than the administrative
avenue. Going to court is expensive, as it requires lawyers

(although they may help you pro bono – see page 222), and is more time-consuming than administrative action.

All that said, there might be good reasons for a citizen lobbyist to go to court. Sometimes petitions, complaints and meetings are not enough. Court cases can be a powerful way to draw attention to your issue and, by revealing the failings of decision-makers, to bring about change through the establishment of a legal precedent. They can also halt the progress of the policy or administrative process, and that may suit your purposes. Occasionally, taking the judicial route is a strategic choice even when you have little chance of winning (hence the term 'strategic litigation').

For a citizen lobbyist, winning a court case is a big deal. You may expose or even stop an injustice, highlight the wrongdoing of decision-makers, or win compensation. Yet litigation rarely gives you the means to achieve your ultimate goal as a citizen lobbyist. Rather, it is one of the tools – if one of the most powerful ones – in the process of bringing about change. Strategic litigation is generally used in combination with other avenues.

So, when would the judicial avenue be a strategic choice?

Unlike conventional litigation, strategic litigation is not solely in the applicant's interest, but pursues a broader social issue. Since winning a court case means setting a legal precedent, this outcome will benefit many other individuals who find themselves in the same situation. In other words, strategic litigation is set to affect your issue in ways that go well beyond the outcome of the dispute. This explains why you may decide to go down the judicial avenue even when your chances of success are small or non-existent. In other words, you only go 'judicial' when the strategic advantage you may obtain outweighs the costs. Your likely opponents will know this too. Companies, but also public authorities, typically favour out-of-court settlements rather than court rulings. They prefer to pay considerable amounts of money to you rather than publicly face your claims, since a court case could be highly damaging for them.

The advantages of strategic litigation may consist of:

- drawing public attention to your issue;
- bringing injustice to light;
- stopping an injustice;
- forcing an advantageous delay;
- embarrassing the decision-makers;
- prompting and/or shaping the legislative process to come;
- bringing about a long-lasting social change.

However, going to court to advance your lobbying campaign might be a bit of a stretch. The purpose of courts is to solve disputes, not to address wider policy issues. That's the job of the elected representatives and their administrative offices.

This explains why you are likely to encounter various obstacles when going down the judicial path. The major impediment are the rules on standing – i.e. your ability to bring a case before a given court. Not everyone can go to court. It requires not only a strategic analysis but also a reality check, in terms of the time and effort necessary to succeed. Supporting someone else's legal claim in exchange for a share of the potential damages has become big business. The people who fund your legal claim can sometimes make a profit (depending on your country) by taking a share in the proceeds of successful claims.

STORY – Max Schrems Takes on Facebook

Take the example of Max Schrems, which we first encountered in the Introduction. Max, an Austrian citizen, successfully used the court system to challenge Facebook's data protection regime.

In 2011 Max, then a law student, spent an exchange semester at Santa Clara University in California. There, he attended a presentation on data protection given by Ed Palmieri, Facebook's privacy lawyer, and was so astonished by what he heard that he wrote an academic assignment about it. In August of the same year, back in Europe and convinced that Facebook was acting against EU data protection law, Max decided to file a complaint against Facebook Ireland Ltd – Facebook's European headquarters – with the Irish Office of the Data Protection Commissioner.

The complaint was aimed at stopping Facebook from transferring data from Ireland to the US. The case ended up before the European Court of Justice. Max was found to have been right from the start, and the ECJ ruled in line with his arguments in October 2015. As a result, Max resubmitted his original complaint against Facebook with the Irish Data Protection Commissioner. He also filed a similar complaint to the Hamburg and Belgian Data Protection Authorities. These were designed to enforce the ECJ judgement. Before that ruling, back in August 2014, Max filed another lawsuit against Facebook at a local Viennese court, and encouraged other Facebook users to join his case for free, generating a 'class action'-style suit and gathering 60,000+ supporters via his webpage. This case is now pending before the Austrian Supreme Court.

Throughout the entire process, Max was able to rely on the financial support of the German litigation funder ROLAND ProzessFinanz AG; Max's well-founded arguments convinced them to support him. Max is now finishing a PhD on data protection.

STORY – Irish Language

An Irish-medium language school (that is, a school in which education is provided in the Irish language) in Belfast successfully challenged the Department of Education's failure to put adequate transport arrangements in place. The case was taken forward by Colma McKee, Vice Chairperson of the school's board. He claimed that the Department of Education for Northern Ireland (DENI) had breached its statutory duty to encourage and facilitate education in the Irish language, under Article 89 of the Education (Northern Ireland) Order 1998, by failing to provide adequate transport to pupils in rural areas. The failure meant pupils and would-be pupils of Coláiste Feirste who lived outside Belfast and wished to be taught in the Irish language found it extremely difficult to reach the school.

The High Court found in favour of McKee and concluded that the statutory duty to promote the Irish language was not 'merely aspirational' but rather 'has and is intended to have practical consequences and legislative significance'. It further ruled that the Department of Education '... failed to give proper weight and consideration to its obligation under Art 89 to encourage and facilitate the development of Irish language medium education'. The Court also compelled DENI to give further consideration to the transport issue in the post-primary Irish-medium education sector.

TIP 12 – File an Amicus Curiae Brief

Starting a court case is an audacious move. A way to benefit from the judicial route without necessarily having to lead it is to join a pending dispute on your issue. Given you will have expertise in the issue, it would be a missed opportunity not to play a role in the dispute. One way to help influence its outcome is to file an amicus curiae (literally, friend of the court) brief. An amicus curiae is someone who, although not a party to a case and unsolicited by any of the parties involved, assists the court and offers information with a bearing on the case. Since not all courts accept unsolicited briefs by individuals who are not party to a dispute, you may be able to influence the court simply by circulating your brief – posting it online, as well as sending it to the judges and clerks who are working on the case. Having worked for the highest European court, I know that when outsiders present good arguments they will be taken into account regardless of how they reach the court.

To find out more about how you can fund your litigation, see Step 6: Who Pays.

Public Campaigning

Public campaigning is another avenue for your lobbying. Essentially, it is about building public support and momentum for your cause, and it can have a huge impact on the effectiveness and reach of your campaign. While all lobbyists share the same aim – to put pressure on decision-makers – campaigning pursues this objective without necessarily having to tackle demanding and formal legislative, administrative or judicial processes. Campaigning is by definition an informal way of operating with no need of official approval.

Increasingly, it is used in combination with other activities, such as legislative (e.g. campaigning to support or oppose a legislative proposal) or administrative (e.g. to back a formal petition calling for the closure of a polluting plant) action. Used in conjunction with another avenue, public campaigning amplifies and publicises the issue quickly and more efficiently. Who would ever find out about your official petition without a well-designed campaign? Which decision-maker would care about your issue if no one had heard of it? People don't necessarily want to know *how* you are going to tackle something (e.g. through a new policy or by closing a plant). What they care about is that the change happens.

Even when deployed by itself, campaigning sometimes prepares the ground for further courses of action. After you've mobilised people in a given cause, you may need – if decision-makers don't respond – to channel your support into follow-up actions. This often means pursuing formal avenues, the most privileged of which is petitioning.

A petition is often the start of a long journey. In the UK, half a million citizens signed a petition against a proposal that would have led to the selling-off of England's national forests. A British charity dedicated to political activism, 38 Degrees, ran a poll that revealed 84 per cent of the British public thought forests should remain in public hands. They went on to raise a further £60,000 to put advertisements in national newspapers and apply pressure to an independent panel. This particular journey lasted 27 months, and forced the government to make a U-turn on the issue.[31]

On top of its immediate policy aims, public campaigning also pursues longer-term objectives aimed at changing perceptions. You may want to challenge a stereotype, or make a particular practice socially acceptable. While virtually all the avenues I've discussed can change social norms, by altering how we perceive a given behaviour (such as alcohol consumption, domestic violence or police conduct), this aim is generally better achieved through public campaigning. You can challenge a social norm by proving it wrong, or you can promote it by normalising it. Today, social media campaigns often seek to alter – typically counter – standard media representations as a way of challenging social norms. For instance, if mainstream media continue to portray women as sexual objects in order to sell a product or service, social media users may counter that narrative by turning it on its head.

Let's consider a public campaign that challenged the 'rape culture' that pervades American sporting culture. Samantha

Stendal, a student from the University of Oregon, was angry at the way mainstream media covered a rape trial in which two Ohioan high school American football stars were convicted of raping a sixteen-year old. They had met the young woman at a party when she was drunk. Stendal felt the media helped to normalise their behaviour by focusing on how the convictions would affect the students' sports careers rather than on how the rape affected the girl. She decided to take action by recording a video – together with some friends – aimed at showing how a 'real man' would behave when meeting a woman who has been drinking. The video rapidly went viral and was taken up by mainstream media. As a result, US colleges are now reviewing their regulatory and cultural responses to this intolerable behaviour.

Individuals who find themselves in terrifying circumstances may also campaign by relying on the collection of unofficial signatures to draw the attention of public authorities to their plight. Although their motive is personal, they may lead public authorities to adopt a decision that benefits others in a similar situation. In 2012, Josh, an eleven-year-old with severe autism, was moved from a hospital in Cornwall where his parents live, to another one hundreds of miles away in Birmingham. His parents had been making the trips there for two years every weekend to see him, as they had been told by the NHS that no institution was capable of taking care of Josh closer to their home.

On the advice of a charity, his father Wills, who usually 'doesn't like to rock the boat', decided to start a petition on Change.org. It attracted 10,000 signatures in a week and caught the attention of NHS executives and officials. Wills met Norman Lamb, a former care minister, and then the CEO of the NHS commissioning group in charge of placements, who appointed someone to communicate with the family. They were eventually able to place Josh in day care not far from his home.

Thanks to his petition, Wills forced different bodies that would not otherwise have cooperated to grasp the urgency of the situation. It shows how quickly a petition can concentrate minds and make them think about new scenarios.

As far as citizen lobbying is concerned, campaigning can take place both on- and offline. The former approach relies on things like social media networks and mobile apps, while the latter can include snail mail, street protests, face-to-face meetings and sit-ins. Young people are increasingly adopting any means necessary to change the world.[32]

A good illustration of a smart and effective way to combine on- and offline tactics is a citizen campaign against the mistreatment of animals in abattoirs in France. It was sparked by video footage showing livestock and horses writhing in pain while still conscious, which is against French law.

STORY – French Abattoir Abuse

Since it was founded in 2008, members of the pro-vegan group L214 have been staging shock tactic protests such as animal funeral processions and performance art displays. In 2016, the group attracted national attention when it released a series of undercover videos highlighting the shocking mistreatment of animals in slaughterhouses across the country. The videos went viral and were flagged up by major newspapers. The group launched a website and attracted over half a million followers on Facebook, as well as collecting over 150,000 signatures for a petition demanding transparency in the abattoir industry. The government has been forced to introduce new legislation to penalise guilty owners and put in place protection for industry whistle-blowers. It also announced that it would inspect every abattoir in France.

Despite the rapid growth of digital campaigning and the explosion of social media, the most successful campaigning combines both online and offline tactics. One excellent example is the work of Color of Change, a citizen movement which has become the largest African-American civil rights group in the US.[33] When it launched in 2005, very few people were using email to force the government to act. Today, it has more than 1.3 million members and, like the civil rights movements of the 1960s, Color of Change relies on the power of the media to draw attention to the daily injustices African-Americans experience. In a typical campaign, it asks people to sign petitions, write letters or make phone calls to officials and to post their concerns on various social media channels. In 2009, their campaign against Glenn Beck, a controversial television personality, attracted 285,000 signatures and persuaded 300 advertisers to pull their slots from Fox News, which broadcast Beck's show. As a result, the network removed Beck. In another campaign, Color of Change succeeded in persuading the producers of Saturday Night Live to include black women in the show's cast.

Today the tool of choice for public campaigning is the online petition. Through any of the various online petition platforms – such as Avaaz, Change and WeMove.eu – you can easily solicit and express views on your issue and convey them to the appropriate decision-maker. There is no need to write an email, search for an email address, or ask for a face-to-face meeting. You can do it all from your desk and you will be able to reach virtually anyone with an internet connection. Free from the restrictions demanded by official petitions, these platforms provide a low-barrier entry to activism, allowing any citizen to directly influence policy. They dramatically cut the cost of recruiting supporters and massively expand your geographical scope. Furthermore, you no longer have to simply trust in existing civil society organisations to make their case. You can – even if it is not always a good idea – circumvent them. We discussed earlier how often citizen lobbyists' efforts are discouraged or even resisted by established civil society organisations who claim a monopoly on your issue. Yet elected representatives often complain that they only hear from professional lobbyists, and want to understand their constituents' preoccupations better. Petitioning platforms allow them to hear from more people – and with more diverse opinions – than in the past.

Despite their advantages, digital campaigning and in particular unofficial, online petitions do have serious flaws. Firstly, not all citizens can use them. People without internet access are excluded, and the politically-savvy are disproportionately empowered. This gap is the result not just of the 'digital divide', but also a general lack of confidence in digital engagement and limited understanding of how it works. The ubiquity of digital technology and information overload have made it increasingly difficult to capture people's attention, and engage your audience in meaningful ways. As a result, although digital creative technologies may *seem* accessible, not everyone can take advantage of them.[34] Secondly, bottom-up digital campaigning like an online petition may get in the way of professional advocacy by civil society organisations that might actually be more effective in bringing about change. They run the risk of diluting messages and drawing popular support, media attention and money away from established NGOs.

Thirdly, they can disrupt traditional policymaking and the privileged access NGOs enjoy. Fourthly, since collecting 'likes' or signatures generally fails to bring about real change, it is easy to dismiss as 'clicktivism'.[35] Some worry that the public sphere may pay a price in the long-term for these low-effort forms of activism.[36] And their failure may dispirit the people who find their online petitions and comments ignored.

But there is significant evidence to suggest that the sheer scale of online petitions has had tangible political impacts.

For example, in 2012, an Avaaz petition which attracted 2.8 million supporters led Members of European Parliament to vote down the ACTA treaty as it would have allegedly limited fundamental rights including freedom of expression and privacy. Likewise, popular support for the Right2Water ECI prompted the Commission to remove water from its concessions directive.[37]

STORY – ACTA

The Anti-Counterfeiting Trade Agreement, or ACTA, is an agreement negotiated in the late 2000s that was intended to create new global intellectual property enforcement standards for the internet and its users. ACTA received a lot of criticism due to the lack of transparency around its negotiations and absence of public consultation. According to its opponents, ACTA contained 'several features that raise significant potential concerns for consumers' privacy and civil liberties, as well as pose threats to digital innovation and the free flow of information on the internet'.[38] Despite this, the agreement was signed by the EU and 22 member states in January 2012. However, due to the public outcry, several of these member states raised concerns shortly afterwards and declined to ratify ACTA. Following the Avaaz petition, the European Parliament declined to give its consent to ACTA in July 2012. India and Brazil were invited to join, but refused due to its lack of popular support. So far, only Japan has ratified the treaty. Thanks to citizen lobbying, within six months of its signing, ACTA was politically dead.

STORY – An EpiPen®omenon

Mellini Kantaya is no professional lobbyist, nor a lawyer or a politician. She is an actress whose husband has an allergic condition. Insurance pays for his medicines in full. In early 2016, she made a lot of noise by lobbying Mylan, a US pharmaceutical firm that had hiked the price of the

EpiPen by nearly 500 per cent in twelve years. There was no apparent reason for this increase, apart from the company's monopoly (see Step 1: Choosing your Battle). Mellini was struck by this abuse of market power when she heard from a Facebook friend whose child suffered from life-threatening allergic reactions. She was facing a $600 bill to pay for two of these pens, which inject a pre-emptive dose of epinephrine.

To try to fight against these price hikes, which forced the poorest and neediest to pay huge sums to pharmaceutical firms, Mellini started a petition entitled 'Stop the EpiPen price gouging' and launched a digital campaign. She posted it on the dedicated online service petition-2congress.com, which sends your petition to the right mailboxes so that it reaches actual lawmakers.

What followed is a perfect example of the power of petitions and social networks combined: in just 45 days her petition was signed 80,000 times, and signatories had sent more than 120,000 letters to congressmen. By that time, staffers from Hillary Clinton's and Bernie Sanders' teams had already called Mylan's CEO, Heather Bresch, who bowed under the pressure and increased the rebates offered to the most disadvantaged. But that wasn't enough.

This wave of popular support soon reached Robyn O'Brien, a long-time activist in the field of allergic conditions, who reposted it to her hundreds of thousands of followers. It then reached the ears of another activist, whose fourteen-year-old son had died from an allergy. This, sadly, fulfilled the fourth rule of petitioning: get people emotionally involved. The issue continued to snowball, until Sanders himself condemned the gouging on Twitter, explaining why the pharmaceutical giant's behaviour could not go unchecked (third box checked).

As I write, Mellini's petition has now attracted more than 40,000 signatures and Congress has launched a Commission enquiry into the price of EpiPens, which is likely to make them less expensive. So a petition is only a start, and advocacy still has to follow.

Be aware that – with rare exceptions – you won't be allowed to pursue the 'administrative avenue' using an unofficial petition. In other words, you are generally not permitted to channel the signatures into official petition systems. They could, however, become one of the major tools of your public campaign.

Regardless of how you intend to use them, informal petitions allow you to collect signatures at no cost, although some platforms may charge for certain services such as promoting the petition on your homepage, or granting access to the full list of signatures.

For organisations creating one-off or infrequent petitions, these tools provide a simple and easy-to-use solution, but only basic petition functionality. Use these sites with care. Make sure you're able to export data about your supporters from the website, check that the costs are set out upfront, and ensure that the site doesn't retain the right to email the people who sign your petition. They will often regard this as spam.

Popular platforms include:

Avaaz (Avaaz.org)
Avaaz is the largest activist site in the world, and takes its name from the Farsi word for 'voice'. Operating in seventeen different languages, the platform counts over 41 million

members who have signed at least one of its many petitions. Topics range from human rights abuses in Burma and FGM in Somalia, to war in Syria and African elephant poaching. His founder is my friend Ricken Patel.

WeMove (wemove.eu)
With nearly 400,000 members, WeMove is the new kid on the block. It aims to bridge the gap between European citizens and their representatives in Brussels by acting as a pan-European tool for linking together NGOs and online campaigning platforms.

38 Degrees (38degrees.org.uk)
Founded in the UK by a group of campaigners who were 'determined to do something different', 38 Degrees has 3 million members. As well as hosting petitions on its website, the group prides itself on holding MPs to account by actively pressuring them both in person and online.

SignOn (signon.org)
Recently developed by MoveOn.org, SignOn is still in the beta testing stage, but provides a simple, free petition tool that lets you download the list of names as a PDF file. This is useful when it comes to delivering the petition, but less so for a pledge.

Change.Org (change.org)
This popular and simple tool allows you to create a petition for free, but charges a fee for exporting or downloading the final

list. It does have a sizeable, active community, which makes it an attractive option if you want more reach.

The Petition Site (thepetitionsite.com)
One of the oldest online petition tools, this site run by Care2 offers free basic features which are similar to those available on Change.org, but charges fees to promote the petition or download names.

Causes (causes.com)
Best-known as a fundraising tool, this site provides some basic petition and pledging functions. Causes is integrated with Facebook and therefore easy for its users to pass on, which is a useful feature for those with active audiences there.

When you choose an independent online platform, be sure to pick the one that matches your aims and resources. The map on the next page sets out their different features.

Effective public campaigns must be able to mobilise their supporters – both digitally and in the real world. Collecting 'likes' or signatures usually fails to bring about real change and is easy to dismiss as clicktivism. Public campaigning requires 'deeper' forms of engagement. Yet converting digital attention into meaningful action is not easy. The exercise risks sliding back into the old trap of powerlessness: people may end up passively taking in a campaign rather than acting upon it. The internet has made it easier than ever to find other, like-minded individuals, but it is also makes it harder to join together in a common goal. We send out more noise than

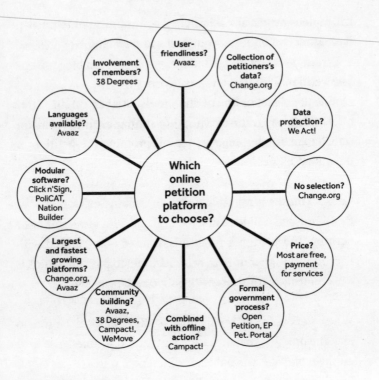

© Alberto Alemanno

signal. The very same (digital) tools that ought to empower us end up controlling our lives instead.

Campaigning, like any other avenue, demands a targeted approach and a careful choice of the tools that will best promote your aims. To make things even more challenging, media exposure is becoming harder to control. Information jumps between networks. A campaign you may have prepared for one audience and one purpose may be accessed by a completely different set of people. This is often described as 'context collapse': an infinite number of contexts collapse into a single moment of content creation, be it a blog post or a video.[39] While this means your message can reach almost anyone, it also makes it vulnerable.

For a more detailed look at digital campaigning tools, see Step 7: Communication.

TIP 13 – When to Launch an Online Petition

Official petitions vs unofficial petitions: the things to consider

1. Official petitions are procedurally constrained, unofficial are not. As a result, their geographic, policy and target scope is virtually limitless. However, the official ones generally guarantee a response from public authorities. The unofficial do not.

2. Official petitions do not allow their creators to contact or mobilise the signatories to urge them to take more action. Unofficial ones do.

From an internal management perspective, it is easier to rely on unofficial platforms as they provide you with many opportunities to engage your supporters and take further action. However, their support won't be immediately channelled into a formal procedure.

STEP 5: Pick Your Allies

'A single bracelet does not jingle.'
Congolese proverb

'You can't stay in your corner of the forest
waiting for people to come to you. You
have to go to them sometimes.'
A.A. Milne, *Winnie the Pooh*

Once you have your positional maps and an overall lobbying plan, you should be able to work out whom to contact in order to persuade them to join you. There are several advantages in building a coalition around your issue: the more diverse your team, the greater its reach. But coalitions can have downsides, especially when they extend to professional organisations whose staff are – unlike you – paid for doing their job.

The most important reason to build a coalition is that it will have a greater impact. The more broad-based your coalition, the more likely you are to attract policymakers' attention. We live in increasingly polarised societies in which issues that are promoted (or merely supported) by one side of the political divide are often automatically opposed by the other. However, if you can attract bipartisan political support, your chances of success will inevitably increase. And the more supporters you manage to mobilise, the deeper your outreach will be. This is because by mobilising more actors, you boost your opportunities to appeal to people who relate to the issue, or who are influential in their own communities. For example, in my alcohol marketing campaign, we could team up exclusively with like-minded health promotion organisations, or we could widen our base and encourage associations for the victims of car accidents and domestic violence to get on board.

Be open-minded. Companies may and should be brought on board if they can add value without undermining the legitimacy of your campaign. For this reason, you should consider putting together a cross-sectoral coalition (often defined as an 'unconventional' coalition), involving people and organisations from the business community, the public sector and other NPOs. It might be the right time for you to approach companies to test their appetite for supporting your lobbying action. In their drive for social responsibility, a few companies like Mary Kay, Royal Dutch Shell and General Motors are leveraging their deep pockets, government contacts and powers of persuasion for the greater good.[40] While it is NPOs that typically promote social issues, as Kyle Peterson and Marc Pfitzer explain, corporations, 'with their carefully cultivated connections, wider lobbying leeway and proficiency in influence, are often better equipped to make the case for stopping domestic violence, improving safety on the roads, thwarting climate change and fostering economic development – to name just a few social change efforts.'[41]

A growing number of companies are trying to prove that corporate advocacy need not always be self-interested. If your cause aligns with their corporate social responsibility efforts, they might be willing to get on board.

Mary Kay Inc., a large marketing and direct sales company that sells cosmetics products, is an example of a company that has used its contacts in government to lobby for good.

Since the 1980s, it has worked to protect women from violence in the United States by focusing on domestic violence prevention programmes. Rather than just making donations, the company has lobbied the US government for more than $500 million in additional federal funds to combat domestic violence, sexual assault and stalking. As well as teaching its cosmetics' sales force about the issue, the company has educated legislators about domestic violence through its lobbying department. Combined with the advocacy of dozens of other groups, including many NPOs, Mary Kay's efforts paid off: President George W. Bush signed the extra funds into law in January 2006.

When looking for potential corporate allies, don't focus exclusively on corporate social responsibility leaders. A growing body of research suggests that the companies that are willing to team up with not-for-profits and grassroots organisations in advocacy campaigns, in particular boycotts, are typically not known for being socially responsible.[42] You will indeed soon find out that the companies keener on working with you are those who do so as a publicity exercise or as an opportunity to gain protection against future challenges and actions. While this instrumental motive might put you off, research backed up by my own experience suggests that these companies, upon joining advocacy campaigns, often develop a genuine interest in the issue that you have proposed them to address.[43] A defensive motive might soon turn into a genuine effort to be at the vanguard of social activism.

This is an important take-away that you should seriously consider. In your coalition-building efforts, always be ready to contact the second-worst offender before launching a campaign. You may want to say 'either we are going to target you or the company worse than you. We believe you don't what to be the one that it is targeted, and we would like to partner with you'. By the way, the very same strategy also works in campaigns targeting public authorities. Give them some healthy competition!

Having said that, let me caution you before you move to enter a corporate partnership. While you may gain from closer ties with companies, both managerially and financially, the risk of your campaign being co-opted by them must not be overlooked. This might prevent you from achieving your own mission and might tarnish your legitimacy. In other words, you must be careful in picking up the right corporate partners.

The second advantage of coalition-building is as a source of further ideas, resources and knowledge for your cause. A coalition is made up, by definition, of actors that differ in status, size, influence and resources. You and your core team may be joined by some non-profit groups, perhaps some experts and even a few companies. Each coalition member, whether a group or an individual, brings to the coalition community a different perspective and can pick up different tasks. Some might work on research, others on communication, others on a new website. Each plays a different role according to their expertise and resources.

It is vital from the beginning to agree on the rules governing co-operation between the members. In particular, it is a good idea to draw up a coalition action plan setting out:

- a timeline for the lobbying action, and the steps that need to be followed;

- the core members, often called the 'steering committee', which is generally entrusted to take decisions under self-imposed rules (e.g. voting rules, prerogatives, etc.);

- who is responsible for which parts of the lobbying plan;

- the contact person, i.e. the person representing the coalition to policymakers and the outside world;

- the spokesperson, i.e. the person entrusted to speak to the media.

Whatever you do, you must ensure that when you draw up these rules, each group has a say in the process and gains full ownership of your action. To be worthwhile, a coalition needs reliable and committed members. As previously mentioned, it is particularly useful to count among them some members of your lobbying target. Politicians care when their constituents contact them because they, unlike the rest of the population, vote and determine not only their future political survival but also their ability to serve the greater good. You must, however, resist the temptation to include people who – although very influential – have not officially agreed to join your coalition. It might be tempting to exploit their popularity, but you may end up paying a price for it by losing control of your action. This situation can backfire and undermine your work, as well as that of the other coalition members. Avoid, avoid, avoid!

TIP 14 – Coalition Members' Inventory

To tap into the full potential of your coalition, you must draft a members' inventory. For each group member, this should include an indication of the number of active members, their contact lists, the communication channels they use (email, social network, mailing list, dedicated intranet) and how often they are in contact. The purpose of the inventory is to determine how many people can be reached through the coalition. This number matters both for internal reasons (more resources) and external ones (weight and representativeness of the action).

By combining networks, some of the people contacted might make a big contribution to the coalition and boost its reach. Some may want to act as ambassadors, others might host information meetings, others may collect signatures (in the case of a petition). Like the factsheet, the inventory must speak for your action. Make sure you come up with a neat, succinct and memorable document. It must carry clear headings/branding, use a neat font size and bullet points as well as box-outs. Don't hesitate to ask a graphic designer to transform your Word document into an appealing double-sided sheet capable of drawing attention to your cause.

STEP 6: Who Pays?

'You can't expect to hit the jackpot if you
don't put a few nickels in the machine.'
Flip Wilson

You don't need funding to become a citizen lobbyist. Indeed, while fundraising is usually essential to the overall running of a campaign, it is not a requirement for all citizen lobbying actions. Unlike professional lobbying, citizen lobbying actions chiefly rely on volunteers and low-budget solutions. Yet, while volunteering can work wonders, you might encounter some costs. Depending on the nature, scope and extent of the action, you might need to raise money from friends and family, and perhaps need some seed money to cover some of the costs you might encounter. Putting together a campaign plan, and estimating the costs for each element, will provide a clearer sense of your fundraising goal.

Various things can help you keep costs under control. Relying on pro bono advice is one of them. Given the rapid expansion of pro bono, it is becoming easier to identify not only lawyers, but also other professionals who could devote time to your cause. They do not necessarily have to join your core team or even entirely share your mission to give you some free advice. Lots of platforms match organisations seeking help with volunteers. They are active in many parts of the world and belong to the Global Pro Bono Network (see page 301).

ACTIVITY 7 – Look for Pro Bono Help

Identify a volunteering matching platform in your country. To do so, you may want to rely on the Global pro bono directory compiled by the Taproot Foundation.[44] It lists more than 50 skill-sharing volunteering platforms in more than 40 countries around the world.

Even when you succeed in finding a dream team of pro bono volunteers to help with the most technical and expensive tasks, you may still encounter some costs. Even if your lawyers agree not to charge you, they can't save you from other expenses such as filing fees, evidence collection, or transport to court.

The question, therefore, is how to finance your action.

Several opportunities are open to you, ranging from crowdfunding to fundraising via philanthropy. You can raise money online with a donation tool, fundraising events or selling branded merchandise. However, given the project-based nature of your action, the most promising and popular tool to fund citizen lobbying is crowdfunding. This is a way of funding a project or venture by raising financial contributions from a large number of people. It generally takes place via a generic fundraising platform, such as Kickstarter, Indiegogo or RocketHub, or a platform dedicated to civic initiatives, such as ioby and Citizenvestor (US), Spacehive (UK), Catarse (Brazil) and Goteo (Spain). Some civic crowdfunding platforms are even more specialised. Julia Salasky, a former associate at the international law firm Linklaters, found an innovative way to help communities channel their energy and finances in the UK through what she calls 'the little guy who is brave enough to bring a case'. It is called Crowdjustice. It enables individuals, groups and communities to come together to fund legal action. Here, the funders are donors rather than investors, as is often the case in third-party funding litigation.

As civic crowdfunding projects aim to serve the public good, as opposed to funding a commercial project, they are often closely linked with existing, offline relationships. The most frequent mistake is to believe that by simply posting your project online you can bring in money. You need to engage with the public by using many other communication tools if you are going to persuade them to fund you.

You may want to consider fundraising outside of these channels, as Indiegogo, Kickstarter or any of the successful crowdfunding websites will levy a fee (for instance, Kickstarter charges 5 per cent). Instead, you can set up your own crowdfunding structure by incorporating it into your webpage. You may want to do this if you run a successful website or blog, or are capable of attracting potential supporters to your own site. There are several ways in which you can promote a crowdfunding campaign, and these methods are particularly important when your project is being hosted on your own site, for instance, creating Facebook, LinkedIn and Twitter accounts, pages or groups. These are key to the success of your campaign, but you need to regularly update them. Networks that you are already involved with are a good base from which to spread the word, and perhaps even to recruit people to help contribute to the project, if there are any openings.

Think too about recording a video and incorporating it into your website; this will help you promote the campaign by increasing the likelihood that it will be clicked on and shared by your followers.

Regardless of whether you go solo or rely on a pre-existing platform, there is some preparation to do before you kick off a crowdfunding campaign. One of the most important things to do is to establish the amount of money you need to raise to make the project a reality. In order to work out this vital figure, you should spend as much time as possible researching every aspect of the production of your project. Then – and only then – should you consider what benefits and bonuses might be available for supporters who pledge more than the standard amount. It is common practice in crowdfunding to incentivise/reward financial donations. In civic crowdfunding, unlike commercial crowdfunding, you are not expected to pay back in the same currency. You can confer titles on your most important supporters or invite them to public events like press conferences or meetings with decision-makers.

Don't forget that civic crowdfunding platforms are not only about collecting money. The ease with which it is possible to attract financial support while at the same time growing your own community of followers is what makes crowdfunding so popular among citizen lobbyists.

TIP 15 – Don't Be Afraid to Ask for Money

Don't be afraid or ashamed to ask for money. You believe in what you're doing and people will respond if you let your passion shine through. The more people you ask, the more they will give. Asking for money, like any other activity, requires some preparation and a few tips.

To make your case to a potential donor, you need to rely on your factsheet and show them:

- what your issue is and why it matters

- what your solution is and why it works

- the evidence backing up your solution

- how strategic and competent you are

- who the beneficiaries of your action are, possibly via real-life stories

- what you need to make it happen

- how easy it is to contribute and make a difference.

STEP 7: Communication and Media Plan

Every single citizen lobbying action, regardless of the chosen avenue, is a battle to win the hearts and minds of other people. You therefore need to communicate effectively and smartly about both the problem and your proposed solution. You want people to visit your website. You want to extend your reach beyond individual visitors and reach different audiences through media coverage. You want, in turn, to influence the public discussion around your issue and, more critically, you want to define the solution. And the existence of social and participatory media means you may also want to use your communication as an opportunity for co-creation and to strengthen your movement's identity. Communication is therefore vital. It is generally – yet not always (think of inside lobbying) – about raising awareness of your issue in society. Sometimes, your communication may entail storytelling: [45] crafting a compelling story about why your issue matters and how it relates to people, which your potential supporters can connect with in an immediate and meaningful way.

Citizen lobbying means communicating with at least three different audiences: decision-makers, the media and the general public. While communication to policymakers and the media requires targeted dissemination (i.e. you choose to communicate some information to key individuals), communication to the general public entails general dissemination. Remember that due to the 'context collapse' of our networked environment (see page 215), it is increasingly difficult to control who will be exposed to your message. Depending on your overall lobbying plan, you must work out not only whom to talk to, but also how and when. Sometimes you will also have to decide who speaks – the 'messenger'. She/he might be a member of your core team (generally the spokesperson), a coalition member or somebody else, such as a celebrity.

In any event, your communications plan, which may encompass different media – generally a combination of targeted and general dissemination tools – must be in line with both your research findings and lobbying plan. It therefore builds on your factsheet and adapts that information to different audiences.

Communication of your issue and proposed action may take many forms, including dissemination via:

- *mainstream media* via opinion pieces, letters, interviews or citations in articles;

- *unconventional media* via blog posts, self-publishing websites (e.g. Medium, Facebook, LinkedIn), or videos (e.g. on YouTube);

- *paid advertisement*, offline or online;

- dedicated, *network-based channels*, such as a Facebook group page, mailing list, YouTube channel, etc.;

- *press releases;*

- *education and dissemination materials*, such as leaflets, posters, infographics, gadgets and even graffiti;

- *events*, such as press conferences, workshops, hackathons and 'unconferences';

- *publication of your formal actions*, such as complaints, court briefs or petitions.

One of the most successful ways to communicate about your cause is through infographics. These are charts or diagrams used to represent information or data, and may be tailored to difference audiences. As is often said, a good infographic is worth a thousand words.

When you merely want to raise awareness about your issue, you may prepare a few banners, images containing a catchy message.

Regardless of the medium chosen, every attempt at communicating about your issue must address these questions:

- *target*: who is the target audience?
- *content*: what information should be shared?
- *context*: where will communication take place?
- *aim*: why am I making this presentation?
- *design*: how can I make the presentation work?

Every single factor must be considered as you frame your message. A message aimed at the general public demands plain language and easy-to-understand content; the same message targeted at a specific audience, such as a decision-maker, will need to be detailed, fact-based and more substantial. The former may be an advertisement, an infographic or a leaflet; the latter may be a policy report, a legislative amendment or an administrative complaint. In any event, you must be clear about the message that you want to convey, tailor the information to the audience and always conclude it with a call for action.

As you draw up your communications plan, you should establish a timeline for your outreach efforts. A well-planned media campaign requires staged releases of information over time. While generating your own publicity is vital at the beginning of your action, you might soon need the help of third parties, such as newspaper correspondents, TV journalists or bloggers, to get your issue packaged and conveyed to a wider public. Be ready to have all you need to communicate and handle your subsequent media relations.

By now you should have prepared all your communications content and be ready to get it out! It's time to focus on some of the major communications steps below to help you hone your plan.

ACTIVITY 8 – Draw up a Communications Plan

Pick a combination of the various forms of dissemination that will best convey your message! Keep in mind who your communication targets are and the key information they need in order to act.

Branding

The first communications challenge for any lobbying campaign is to find an appropriate name (or branding). It must be catchy, snappy and memorable. How you brand your issue to the outside world plays a key role not only in how well it will 'sell' in the marketplace, but also on how your issue will be defined in the public debate. At different points in your campaign, the brand may be critical – from the initial contact-making phase, to coalition-building and the search for funding. It can build trust and enhance credibility.

The purpose of branding is captured in a model called the Role of Brand Cycle. In this model, the brand is embedded within a lobbying strategy, which in turn is embedded within the mission and values driving the action. Branding plays a variety of roles that, when performed well, link together in a virtuous cycle. A well-aligned identity and image position the group, sometimes a coalition, to build internal unity and trust among external actors. The resulting reputation then enhances the identity and image of the brand with which the cycle began.

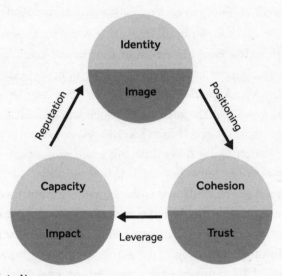

© Alberto Alemanno

From the brand cycle model, it should be clear that a brand is more than a name, logo or graphic design used by a group or organisation. It is more than just a visual identity. A brand, as explained by Nathalie Kylander and Christopher Stone, is 'a psychological construct held in the minds of all those aware of the branded action'.[46] But why does citizen lobbying need to make psychological associations through branding?

While lobbying is first and foremost about influencing decision-makers to do (or oppose) something, it involves – like any other form of social interaction – catching people's attention. The branding must be in line with the overall lobbying plan and, like any other form of communication, must take into account the various audiences you're targeting. If you're simply trying to collect signatures, you'll need snappier and simpler branding than if you want to persuade decision-makers of the merits of a legislative amendment.

Framing your issue to appeal to the right section of the public is key. A good brand should cast your issue in a new light so it will grab the attention of people who would not normally notice it. A good brand galvanises support and conveys an aspiration, but it takes time and some effort to come up with good ones. Some brands do this beautifully.

Make Poverty History is the biggest ever anti-poverty movement, calling for the total cancellation of bad debts owed by poor countries. The phrase highlights its ambitions in an easy-to-understand way.

TckTckTck represents an unprecedented network of more than 400 NPOs led by the Global Campaign for Climate Action (GCCA), which was formed to influence the international climate change treaty at the 2009 UN Climate Change Conference in Copenhagen. The 'tck tck tck' brand evokes time ticking away, underlying their core message that we need to take immediate action on climate change.

#BlackLivesMatter had existed as a phrase for some time, but it was not until 2013 that it spread widely on social media, following reports of police brutality towards black people in Ferguson, Missouri and elsewhere, and subsequent civil unrest. It became a popular Twitter hashtag and turned into a movement after George Zimmerman was acquitted of murder, after shooting African-American teen Trayvon Martin. Black Lives Matter gained public salience through its street demonstrations before it became a fully-fledged organisation. The wider Black Lives Matter movement, however, is a decentralised network with no formal hierarchy. #BlackLivesMatter was tweeted more than 9 million times in 2016, and the hashtag has become a calling card for social justice and racial equality activists across the US.

TIP 16 – Branding for Coalition

Always think strategically about how to name and brand your campaign.

Branding in a coalition is tricky because there is a risk that the new name may overshadow NPOs' or even corporations' existing branding. More broadly, there can be tensions between brand protection and the risks inherent in advocacy. Avoid this by ensuring you have an open and inclusive debate with your coalition members when you pick the brand for the campaign. Never forget branding's original aim: to help you devise a name, frame and package for your issue which will make it immediately recognisable and memorable to the public.

Storytelling

> 'We do not need magic to change the world, we
> carry all the power we need inside ourselves
> already: we have the power to imagine better.'
> J.K. Rowling

Storytelling is a powerful way of drawing attention to your issue. It is a vital tool for engaging supporters, donors and funders, and must be one of the key components of your communication plan. Everyone in your team needs to be able to tell a compelling story about why your issue matters and how it relates to people.

Once you have settled on a brand identity, storytelling is the next step of your communications plan.

A personal, compelling story adds life to a complex issue or a rather dry policy-based campaign. Often a good story can overcome prejudice, undermine preconceptions and shift attitudes towards an intractable issue or vulnerable group that is routinely dehumanised, stigmatised or ignored. When your story is a personal one that springs from your own experience, it has even greater potential to move people and encourage them to confront injustice. Finally, telling stories can empower somebody affected by the issue by giving them a voice and recognising their expertise.

Be careful to distinguish between storytelling and first-hand testimony, although there may be overlap between the two. Each has its own pros and cons. Storytelling can be done by anyone in your group; first-hand testimony means the speaker must have direct experience of the story, which gives your message more authenticity. Telling a story second-hand carries less emotional potential, but is easier to control.

Of course, you can extrapolate your storytelling from first-hand testimony. For instance, when we were lobbying for legislation to protect whistle-blowers in Europe, Antoine Deltour, possibly the most prominent European whistle-blower at that time, was invited to speak in front of the European Parliament to tell his story. The story he told combined his own experience (his first-hand testimony) with a persuasive case for establishing a legislation protecting whistle-blowers. That's an example of the use of storytelling at public events and hearings. Usually, however, you will be telling a story through written and visual materials.

There are many ways to put together a story for your advocacy work, but these tips should help.

1. **Pick your audience**: ask yourself who will listen to your story. Only by understanding who you're speaking to will you really connect with your audience. Don't make the mistake of getting into storytelling without identifying clear goals and knowing how you will measure whether they have been met. You need some strategic guidelines to craft the right content. Design an engagement plan using appropriate platforms to reach the right people and mobilise them. This builds upon and enlarges the coalition members' inventory you have previously devised.

2. **Be strategic**: when picking your story, ask yourself which is the best story to tell. Once you know who your target

audience is, you need to start hunting for stories. Collect a few and run them by your friends and colleagues. The one you choose should not only be compelling, but also a good fit for your lobbying campaign. For instance, testimony from a woman who has actually suffered domestic violence will be more compelling than hearing a politician talk about their desk-based efforts to stop it, however relevant.

3. **Build your story**: once you have identified a set of potentially good stories, you need to fact-check them, frame them and transform them into narratives. If it isn't possible to find a real story, you may want to think about writing a fictitious one. This will give you more flexibility and scope, but at the expense of authenticity. Should you opt for this path, make sure to make it clear the story is fictitious.

4. **Choose your medium**: once you have one or more stories to tell, identify the best way to tell them. You could write a blog post, record a video, run an interview, insert the story in your factsheet or a combination of these.

5. **Search for a storyteller**: regardless of whether your story is real or fictitious, you need someone capable of telling it. If you have found a first-hand testimony, reassure the person whose story it is that their efforts can make a real difference. Sometimes you find an exceptional story but the person involved is not willing to appear. In this case,

try to save the story and find ways to anonymise the story-teller and/or the story itself. If the story is fictitious, your storyteller must be credible and ready to prepare for a video or public appearance. Make sure they are comfortable in the role. Always be aware of the ethical issues that may arise when you bring in someone to campaign for you.

6. **Call to action**: make sure you leverage the story's emotional appeal with a final call to action. Tell the audience what they can do to get involved. As always, the KISS rule applies: keep it simple, stupid![47]

Storytelling reminds you that your issue is about real people, not PowerPoint presentations and factsheets.

ACTIVITY 9 – Write Your Story

Put together a one-page storyline to support your issue.

Media Campaign

Unlike professional lobbying – which typically takes place behind closed doors – the vast majority of citizen lobbying avenues require some form of communication with the general public. We often call it media advocacy, and like any other form of lobbying it must be strategic. Companies may have something to lose (generally in terms of brand reputa-tion) from speaking out about their issue. Citizens like you don't. So you need to devise a media campaign as part of your broader communications plan. This is a planned series of media appearances. It may involve newspaper or website articles, TV interviews, press releases and social media.

Generally, the most immediate aim is to generate cover-age for your issue and help define it. But you should always ask yourself what you are trying to accomplish. Sometimes the goal is simply to raise awareness (of domestic violence or teenage pregnancy, for example). Yet you probably want to nudge people towards specific action – signing a petition, joining a protest or taking public transport instead of the car, for example.

A good media campaign is vital for at least three reasons. Firstly, the more people know about your issue, the more likely you are to win their support. You can't imagine how often I receive emails, tweets and LinkedIn messages express-ing support after a blog post, op-ed piece or TV appearance covering an issue I'm working on. The people who write: 'I read about this issue and feel that something must be done about it' might even join your core team and become your closest lobbying allies. Some write to me saying: 'I have been working for 20 years on this issue and would like to contribute to your campaign.' Others might express private support, but can't voice it in public. This might be because they work for one of your opponents (whether an industry or a political group), or they are elected representatives who can't risk a public endorsement. Yet their unstated support might still be extremely influential as they work with your opponents. I try to foster links with my opponents' aides, as they often sympathise with my cause. In one case, an aide managed to convince her boss not to resist our proposal. In another, my assistant Benjamin and I wrote several op-ed pieces in leading newspapers calling for action against 'revolving door' appointments. Virtually nobody got in touch afterwards. We were initially disappointed, but then noticed that our call for action had been taken up by a coalition of NGOs – who collected more than 60,000 signatures aimed at stopping the former EU Commission President José Manuel Barroso from joining Goldman Sachs as their Brexit advisor.

Secondly, the more media coverage you attract, the more likely policymakers are to heed your issue because they will spot an opportunity for bolstering their public support. Getting your story covered by the media has a disproportionate effect on the success of your campaign. Everyone, not only decision-makers, will take it much more seriously. It will look more credible and gain heft. Journalist Walter Lippmann famously defined the media as:

> the beam of a searchlight that moves relentlessly about, bringing one episode and another out of the darkness and into vision. Men cannot do the work of the world by this light alone. They cannot govern society by episodes, incidents, and eruptions. It is only when they work by a steady light of their own, that the press, when it is turned upon them, reveals a situation intelligible enough for a popular decision.[48]

Thirdly, given your limited resources, you have more to gain than lose when people start talking about you. As George Monbiot writes in his activist's guide to the media: 'Exploit the media or the media will exploit you!'[49]

To be effective, any citizen lobbying campaign depends on well-disposed news media that can project their influence into the public and legislative agenda. But not all your stories are equally likely to be picked up in the mainstream media. Journalists and their editors may decide not to follow up on your pitch. Fortunately, you no longer need to rely entirely on mainstream coverage. Facebook and other social media platforms give you the ability to make an impact by promoting your branding, testing your storytelling and eventually circulating content in different media. This is often called transmedia activism.[50] The beauty of it is that it offers your core groups and supporters the opportunity to co-create your message. This may then be taken up by various broadcast media – but even if it isn't, you will have made a valuable contribution to your own issue by building an audience and promoting your cause.

In any event, while media coverage is good for your issue, you have to ensure you remain in control of the message you want to convey. That's why planning a proper media campaign – rather than leaving things in the hands of reporters – is so important. What you can offer to the media is often known as 'information subsidy'. Although businesses and corporate actors tend to provide this subsidy more often than civil society, citizens can also play the game. By relying on your research (Step 2) and outside experts who can speak to the media on your behalf, you may become a source the media will turn to when they cover your issue.

A media campaign should be prepared in advance, and consist of the following major steps:

a. Map the media
b. Spot the journos
c. Build a relationship
d. Draft a press release
e. Prepare for an interview.

Map the Media

Before reaching out to media outlets with your content, you need to draw up an inventory. These might include national (and local) newspapers, radio, TV, online media and magazines. You should identify the news pages, columns, programmes and featured stories that would be a good fit for your story.

Spot the Journos

Once you have a list of the main media outlets, you need to find the journalists who actually run them. These are the people most likely to actually cover your story. Don't pitch to a tech reporter about animal welfare. Look instead for reporters who are likely to be interested in your story because they have covered it before. Tell them why your issue matters by giving them the facts, and pitch yourself as someone with expertise in it. Always be polite to them, even when they don't respond to your emails, don't like your activity or don't follow you on Twitter.

Build Relations

Once you have identified the right journalists, you need to build a relationship with them. They need to gain your trust. This takes time, so you should start cultivating a relationship with them well before you try to 'sell' them your story. You and your colleagues are well-placed to do so given the expertise you have accumulated in the issue. The journalist might want to tap into your expertise and remember you as someone to be quoted as an expert or authority on your issue.

Draft a Press Release

Writing a press release is the best way to 'sell' your story to the media while controlling the message. The document should speak journalists' language, and its presentation should therefore mimic the format and style of a promising news story yet to be written. This will significantly increase your chances of being understood, and reduce the risk of misinterpretation.

The press release should strategically build on the factsheet. It is about reframing your initial research work – we call it repackaging – and selling it to the reporters so as to define the issue in the public's mind.

Here are some tips on how to draft it:

- *Be concise*: a single page document will suffice. If it's any longer, it means you're probably not getting it right;

- *Be clear*: start with a punchy headline (just a few words to catch the journalist's attention), followed by a one-sentence statement summing up the whole storyline;

- *Be fact-based*: the rest of the text should provide the basic facts, evidence and figures underpinning the issue and the solution you put forward in language free of jargon;

- *Be newsworthy*: don't advertise the lobbying itself, but share something *new* of potentially general interest; don't tell more than one story at the time, as it won't be understood and you risk wasting future opportunities to tell other stories;

- *Sign it*: always provide a contact to whom enquiries should be directed (email and/or phone) and list your coalition members.

Once the press release is ready to go live, it is up to you to make sure it will be picked up. Do not get carried away and send it to all your contacts as soon as it's ready. The temptation to do this is very strong – I've experienced it. Yet you must force yourself to be strategic about when, how and to whom to send it. Here a few golden rules on how to circulate a press release:

- *Announce it first*: give a few days' notice (generally a couple of days does the trick) before the scheduled release of a related event. Drawing on your inventory of media outlets and individual contacts, target your press release to specific individuals;

- *Embargo it*: sometimes you may want to instruct the journalists not to release (publish or broadcast) the information in the press release before a certain time. This is generally called an 'embargo' and presents some important advantages: it creates a sense of event around your issue, it reassures journalists that they won't be beaten to the story by others and you remain in control of the moment of the release and can act accordingly;

- *Target the right people*: you should normally target multiple media at the same time – but make sure you choose wisely;

- *Send reminders*: journalists' attention varies and tends to be unpredictable. Don't hesitate to send them the press release up to three or four times before the final release. You can also consider a follow-up email with some journalists you personally know;

- *Follow up*: make sure you provide the media with a follow-up on how your announcement has been greeted by decision-makers, other media and the public.

Remember the effectiveness of citizen lobbying depends on adequately exploiting the news media in order to project their influence into the public and legislative agenda.

TIP 17 – How Readable is Your Press Release?

To ensure your press release is fit for purpose, make sure the headline and one-sentence statement summing up your storyline have covered all the five Ws:

Who, Why, What, When and Where. If it doesn't, start again. Depending on the complexity of your issue, you might consider including a few notes on the back of your one-page document targeting journalists. These extra lines may give you the opportunity to share more information and details about the rationale of your action. Never forget that this is your chance to get people interested in your issue, and you don't want to waste it.

Prep for an Interview

Interview requests are generally unexpected, but they shouldn't catch you unprepared. Make sure you have 'talking points' prepared, so you remain in control of the message you want to convey. Use your press release and stick to it so as to avoid inconsistency and confusion. You need to be prepared and ready to look more knowledgeable than the interviewer; that's where you can score points. If the journalist wants you to take a stance on a difficult or controversial point raised by your opponent, be proactive. Don't let the interviewer box you into in a corner. You have a few options: if you feel like it, you can give a quick answer then move on to what you want to talk about; another, bolder option is to undermine the factual content of the question and provide your take. A final and less desirable approach is to avoid responding to it entirely by quickly switching to: 'Well, the real question is...' Being proactive is generally the best way to save you from embarrassment. We all know how frustrating it is when politicians avoid answering questions directly!

What you should never do is lie. It will inevitably backfire, and you risk losing control of your issue, weakening it and threatening the work of the many people who believe in it.

TIP 18 – Mock Interview

Interviews are expected to be tough. The audience, especially your opponents, will want to see you grilled by the interviewer. Be prepared! Do a mock interview. Ask one of your colleagues to act as the interviewer (you can draw up a list of tough questions) and make sure they give you a hard time. Be ready to record yourself, watch it back and look at what works and which bits need fine-tuning.

Digital Campaigning

The internet has transformed civic engagement and activism and become a vital new avenue of political engagement. For the citizen lobbyist, it is a low-cost channel which allows you to control the quality and quantity of information and organise it in various formats. It enables you, your group and the public to communicate much more easily.

This makes digital campaigning a key asset for you.

Far more people are exposed to political content online than ever participate in offline politics and activism. Digital engagement is fundamentally different, too: it is proactive rather than passive. So it is conducive to political engagement. Connecting with others is inherently empowering, and the links and collaborations the internet enables us to make have the potential to boost civic life. Many people believe social media is improving the democratic process by encouraging more open discussion and greater access to public debate.

Yet this is not always the case. Despite its potential to democratise the political space, the increasing sophistication of apps and online marketing tools can end up limiting our reach. Facebook and Snapchat allow a much more diverse group of people to post on social media. But there is a big difference between posting updates to friends and family, and sharing rich media aimed at a wider public. Nonetheless, while some people are still excluded from the digital revolution, social media are powerful tools – and they can bring the experiences of the marginalised into the mainstream.

The essential online tools for any digital campaign are:

a. Email
b. Social media
c. Online advertising

Email

Email is the tool of choice when it comes to mobilising supporters and raising money. It boasts the highest consistent response rate of any digital medium. Yet it isn't for everyone. Given its intrusive nature, you need to seek your contacts' permission in order to contact them by email. Apps such as MailChimp let you effectively handle and manage significant number of contacts (see Tip 19 below). Text messages have an even higher effective open rate, but are still more intrusive.

Social Media

While email might be the most powerful medium for your digital campaign, it can't do everything. Emailing is private. If someone takes action by following up one of your emails, that exchange is only visible to you and them. Social media, on the other hand, offers a public stage where your supporters' enthusiasm can inspire their friends and family to join in. In that respect, Facebook, Twitter and Instagram score higher than email in terms of engagement.

Moreover, emailing has limits: at some point you will run out of contacts to email. On social media, however, you can post all day long, which gives you constant opportunities to keep your supporters engaged, motivated and involved. If you offer them good content, they will spread the word and do your outreach for you.

Although you should be rightly wary of social media platforms controlled by corporations driven by profit rather than a belief in civic participation, social media can still empower you.

Online Advertising

Online advertising includes not only email marketing, mobile advertising and social media marketing, but also many types of display advertising, such as banner ads. Like 'conventional' advertising, it frequently involves both a publisher (who integrates advertisements into its online content) and an advertiser (who provides the advertisements to be shown there). Technology now lets us target ads based on users' demographic characteristics and recent online behaviour.

Admittedly, none of this is free. But online ads are no longer just the prerogative of large corporations. Facebook and Twitter ads are relatively easy to buy, as are ads on Google Search. DIY advertising platforms exist that can help you devise a digital campaign on social media, and buy banner ads or even video ads targeted directly at potential supporters.

TIP 19 – Do-It-Yourself Digital Campaign

The sheer number of email, social media and online marketing platforms can be overwhelming. The easiest way to get started is to open an account with one of the platforms offering these features:

- Customisable email templates that allow you to design an email in line with your branding and communication strategy;

- Personalisation, with your contact's name in the subject line and throughout the email;

- Analytics to track open rates, click-through rates and overall newsletter success;

- Integration with your social media platforms including Facebook, Twitter, LinkedIn and Google+.

My preferred email marketing platform is MailChimp. It is free for up to 2,000 contacts. You can easily import your past contacts and feed in new ones, even from your own website. MailChimp allows you to preview what your email will look like in any browser and email service before you send it. It's important to test this in order to make

sure it looks good no matter where and how the sub-
scriber reads it.

Blogging

The grassroots, low-cost nature of blogging makes it a particularly good medium for citizen lobbying. Less static and
formal than websites and newsletters, blogs are a great way
to express your point of view about your issue and promote
the work you are doing. The lengthier format allows you to go
into more depth than most other types of social media permit
– yet you can publish new material immediately, and much
more quickly than you can do with a traditional newsletter.

You can either set up and run your own blog (see Tip 20)
or get your posts published by an existing blog. You can even
do both to maximise circulation.

Publishing blog posts on your own site can also improve
its search engine optimisation (SEO) ranking – the order in
which your link pops up in a search engine.

Blogs can have tremendous influence on public opinion.
It was thanks to a post we ran on a couple of blogs that a *New
York Times* journalist approached us and eventually decided to
run a story about our citizen lobbying work calling for reform
of the EU Court of Justice.

Blogging can be used by citizen lobbyists in a number of
different ways:

- To present your issue and proposed solution to the public;

- To build an audience around your issue;

- To popularise your work and make it accessible to a wider audience;

- To monitor and report on new developments;

- To keep your followers and supporters informed;

- To reflect on how to make progress with people who have experience of similar campaigns.

Regardless of your aim, blogging is an increasingly important skill to have. And it can be an excellent way of getting your issue in front of the media while allowing you to remain in control.

ACTIVITY 10 – Blogging

Put together a one-page blog post discussing your issue. Publishing it is not required. You may just want to circulate it among friends and colleagues to get feedback. You can do so by email or through social media.

TIP 20 – Set Up Your Blog

Free hosting sites like WordPress, Tumblr and Blogger make blogs easy to set up and manage. Many design templates are available to manage the blog's appearance and you can pick one to suit your issue and target audience. Blogs can also be hosted on your own website or that of your organisation. Once you have one up and running, make sure you update it regularly – an outdated blog is no use at all. There's not optimal frequency, but a weekly update seems to be common practice. Followers of the blog can sign up to receive new posts when they appear. You can also manage all your followers via MailChimp or another email management site.

Communication Events

While digital dominates the advocacy communication efforts today, offline advocacy should not be underestimated. Events are another way to boost your media campaign. You might organise a press conference, a sit-in or a meet-up for volunteers who want to help your cause. Meet-ups can take many forms: an *ice-breaker* (a chance for volunteers to get to know one another), a *world café* (a structured conversation meant to facilitate frank discussion, and link ideas within a larger group to access the collective intelligence in the room), a *hackathon* (collaborative computer programming), or an *unconference* (an open, participatory workshop-event in which the participants provide the content). For example, your network could kick off with an ice-breaker for participants to get to know each other. It could continue with a world café (sometimes called coffee projects) for a collective reflection, then move on to a hackathon or coding-party (to come up with software) or a flash-mob (for artistic purposes). When you need to feed people, you could organise a 'Disco Soup' – ask your supporters to bring vegetable knives and peelers, get hold of fresh food that would otherwise go to waste, turn on the music and get cooking.[51]

Events like these can help you get your issue in the public eye and mobilise large numbers of people. While a sit-in is generally associated with protesting, events such as hackathons provide a unique opportunity to not only get supporters together but also work on a solution to your issue.

STORY – Burkini Ban

After some French seaside towns banned the 'burkini' – a beachwear garment worn by Muslim women that covers most of the body apart from the face, hands and feet – dozens of British women held a protest outside the French embassy in London in the summer of 2016. Having created a makeshift beach party with tonnes of sand, beach balls and lilos, the demonstrators held up banners criticising the bans. A protest was also held in Berlin. France's High Court lifted the ban shortly afterwards when a human rights organisation took the judicial avenue. Although the decision applied to one of the many French cities on the Riviera that had introduced the ban, the High Court decision is set to lift it completely.

STEP 8: Face-to-Face Meeting

This is the moment you've been waiting for! When your lobbying target invites you, or agrees to meet with you, face-to-face, it feels like a breakthrough. Meeting policymakers in person is the essence of citizen lobbying, and is a vital and ground-breaking moment for your campaign. The meeting is both your opportunity to connect with the decision-maker, and their chance to learn about your issue. Without all your earlier work, coalition-building and communication efforts, you would probably never have made it this far. But don't take this moment for granted. You need to be prepared for it, even though sometimes you might end up talking to an assistant rather than the decision-maker themselves.

Who to Meet

By now, you have mapped all relevant stakeholders and identified your lobbying targets. Your job is to approach the latter, as they are the ones who have the power to bring about change.

So, if you want to support or oppose a proposed law, you must target all the elected representatives (including its opponents) who are going to vote on it. You need to identify the members of the relevant parliamentary (or governmental) committees, as these are the people with the authority to initiate, oppose or even vote on the issue. If, on the other hand, you are lodging a request for access to documents, an administrative complaint or a legal action, you will have to respect the procedures for that particular avenue. Sometimes, a face-to-face meeting is not automatically granted, but can be requested. This is often the case in administrative procedures such as complaints to the ombudsman. You can also ask the relevant people to meet you informally. Public officials tend to be keen to meet, as you can give them useful information that helps them to decide on your issue.

In a legislative process, you want to meet as many elected representatives as possible. In an administrative or political procedure, you will do better to target the key actors. The American DREAM activists (see page 100) successfully met and lobbied Senators John McCain and Harry Reid as part of their campaign. Sometimes you might even consider keeping quiet about your meeting so as not to put too much pressure on the people involved.

The Approach

Once you have identified the key actors, the next step is to approach them. Sometimes the publicity you have generated around your issue may land you an invitation. Generally, though, it will be you who has to take the first step. This means picking up the phone, sending an email and/or leveraging some friends or contacts you have in common so as to arrange a meeting. By now, you are well placed to ask for a meeting: you have done your research and condensed it into a factsheet, you have built a coalition that will give your demand more credibility, and you have publicised the issue, which ideally will have brought it to the attention of the people that matter.

Make sure to prepare the initial approach with the same care as you would take before the actual meeting. Consider what information to share with the decision-makers *before* meeting them. Should you send them the factsheet, the press release or just a cover message? This depends on how well they know the issue. The more they already know about it, the more detailed and to the point your pre-meeting information should be.

You must also consider the information that you want to share *during* the meeting. Bring several extra copies of your factsheet and press release as well as any informative or policy materials you might have prepared. If your campaign has produced a pen, T-shirt or toy, bring them along too: they might entertain your hosts while giving the impression of professionalism. Merchandise or freebies like these tend to stick around in the office of the people you meet.

What surprises my students and fellow citizen lobbyists most is how easy it is to secure a meeting with an elected representative or an official. We regularly pay visits to the European Parliament as well as to national parliaments. While we are often invited to present our work to committees, sometimes we ask both members of parliament and officials to meet us. I often say – to my students' and colleagues' surprise – that it is the duty of politicians and civil servants to meet us, fellow citizens, when doing their jobs. My students' surprise about their welcome speaks volumes about the dire state of our democracies. Meeting officials should be perfectly normal, yet the vast majority of us assume it must be difficult.

Prep the Meeting
You've made it! Your name is in the busy diary of your chosen decision-maker. All your efforts were rewarded. Since you've

worked hard to get all the way here, don't waste it. Revisit your factsheet, prepare a few talking points and be ready to connect with the person you're speaking to.

How do you do this? Empathy – the ability to read people by placing yourself in another's position – will help. Everyone can develop this kind of emotional intelligence.[52] Start by asking yourself: *Why should they be interested in my issue? What's in it for them? Who is supporting whom? Who is (or might be) unhappy if they follow me? Where is the resistance?* These questions might seem obvious, but they are not easy to answer. Sometimes your cleverest opponent may look like a supporter, but he is not supportive at all. He's just smart and knows how to play the meeting game.

Carefully reading people can also help you understand the conflicts that exist in a group. Often these conflicts have nothing to do with your issue or the proposed solution discussed at the meeting. Generally, hidden conflicts and tensions can be traced to very human dynamics: who is allowed to influence whom, the hierarchy among elected representatives and career civil servants, internal wrangling and even personal relationships. Learning how to be empathetic may help you decipher some of these subtle power struggles, and as a result you will be able to spot and manage them.

TIP 21 – Practise Your Empathy

When preparing for the meeting, you can work on your empathy by asking a set of pre-determined questions that might help you connect with your interlocutor at a deeper, personal level. Is there something that the two of you have in common? You might have studied in the same school, have kids of the same age, or have met in the past in a different setting. Ask yourself: Is there something I can do for them (but don't necessarily see yet)? What do they see in me?

Prepare your empathetic connection as much as you can.

The Meeting

You've found your way to the office where the meeting is going to take place. (Make sure you check the location in advance so as to avoid showing up late – that never makes a good impression!) If you can, try to arrive half an hour in advance – that way, you will have time to go for a brief walk and become familiar with the venue, especially if it is your first visit. You might even bump into other influential people for your campaign – though don't lose track of time. I still remember an important meeting which I wasted not only because I arrived late, but also because I showed up sweaty and with my heart pounding. I had bumped into an old friend and caught up with him instead of focusing on the meeting! I'm sure you don't want to throw away all your efforts due to a similar lack of professionalism, right? The good thing about that meeting is that as I was leaving the office, I stumbled upon another big fish and managed to pitch him the issue as well. This earned me another meeting, and I was back in the same building (the European Parliament) the following day. Once you walk the corridors of power, you have an invisible pass … and you ought to use it!

As you are about to go into the meeting, don't forget your story: how did you end up being interested in the issue? What was your 'eureka' moment? How did you succeed in getting other citizens, perhaps organisations and even companies, to rally to your cause? How much effort did it take to get there? Remember that the more authentic your story is, the more powerful your impact will be.

As soon as your host gives you the floor, be ready to thank them and their staff for taking the time to meet you and your team. Your next task is to deliver a brief statement which highlights why your host is well placed – due to their long-standing support or sensibility for the issue – to take the lead, or at least assume a stance. This will give you the chance to show that you are familiar with their previous record and the causes they care about. If you can do this in the first few minutes of the meeting, it can be an excellent way of impressing the elected representative, the official and their respective staff. It needs to be done subtly: your aim is not to flatter, but to score points with your host(s). You should then illustrate your proposed solution by emphasising – via the factsheet – the evidence (key facts and figures) you have gathered, as well as the reasons why they ought to support it. Do your best to present your solution as a win. In the meantime, don't forget to mention and briefly introduce the coalition you have put together, and highlight the number of stakeholders that have signed up.

Don't be disappointed if your host shows little under-standing of the issue (and even less of the solution). During the time you have been working on your issue, they might have been involved in dozens of different initiatives. They might also be a newcomer in the field and have limited experience of it. Sometimes, they just do not enjoy read-ing their files and delegate them to their staff. This is why you should get to know the key staffers and aides who work for your host. Occasionally you may end up learning more about them than you do about their bosses. Staff members can be very influential, and often do most of the work on your issue. Never underestimate their work, though do not necessarily compliment them in front of the decision-maker.

When it comes to the length of the meeting, be flexible. It might be incredibly short but effective, or unexpectedly long and useless. Make sure you leave the meeting with a pending task; you can promise to follow up via email with a particular document, piece of advice or contact so as to keep the con-versation going.

Finally, when you leave the meeting, make sure you remain calm and don't show your feelings – whether you're filled with joy or consumed by disappointment. You can do that in private, but only once you have left the building. While you are still on the premises you may well come across other influential figures. Be prepared to seize the moment with an 'elevator pitch'. This is a short summary that quickly and sim-ply defines a process, product, service, organisation or event and the value it offers.

TIP 22 – Prep Your Elevator Pitch

An elevator pitch is one of the most important preparations you can make. As soon as your issue starts to take shape, think about preparing one. As the name suggests, it should be possible to deliver a succinct summary of what you do in the time it takes to ride in a lift – approximately 30 seconds to a minute.

Imagine you come across someone important in the lift. If the brief conversation that follows is inspiring and meaningful for them, the conversation might continue after the lift ride, or end in the exchange of business cards and a scheduled meeting.

When preparing it, make sure you convey what you do and for whom, and why it is so essential to society. Back up your message with key stats and figures as well as references to your past record.

STEP 9: Monitoring and Implementation

A face-to-face meeting with a decision-maker is a great achievement. Regardless of whether you meet a mayor, an MP or the Prime Minister's chief of staff, it is one of the most rewarding moments of your citizen lobbying experience. But even when you succeed in 'selling' your issue to them and persuading them to act, your battle is not yet over.

In other words, reaching the meeting stage does not exhaust your citizen lobbying efforts. Finding someone willing to share your battle is only the beginning of a new phase, possibly the last, of your work. Now that you have a heavyweight on board, you need to be vigilant about encouraging them to deliver. Make sure that once your issue is in their hands, it progresses in the way you want it to. Regardless of the avenue you pursue, you reach a point at which decision-makers must follow up on your request. They might initiate a new legislative proposal, put forward some amendments to an existing one, adopt an administrative decision or react to a recent judgement. In any of these scenarios, you must strive to not only monitor their progress but also to work closely with the decision-makers so as to influence the process. It would be frustrating to lose control of 'your' issue once you have shared it with an elected representative or administration! Remember, though, that what you want is your issue to be addressed in the most sensible way; it is not about making sure you get all the credit.

Most of the time, keeping tabs on your decision-maker means following the policy cycle through its various stages, from policy initiation all the way to its implementation. Make sure you monitor developments closely even though you are not directly involved in the formal process. To do this, you rely on your contacts as well as on existing media outlets. Google Alerts may help you follow all the relevant documents that have been published online (for a reminder on setting these up, see page 118). If necessary, you can even file an FOIA request in order to get hold of the documents used in the process. Unfortunately, in most countries preparatory documents need not be disclosed.

But there are other things you can do to monitor the decision-making process.

You need to carve out a special role for you and your group in the process in order to make sure the outcome is the one you want. Never forget that if the issue ends up on the political agenda, it is because of your efforts! So you deserve to have the decision-maker's ear. You may be invited to testify as a citizen expert before public authorities, or simply to act as a representative of your group or coalition at a public event. You may be asked to draft wording for the actual policy proposal as the issue goes through the legislative or administrative process. Make sure you apply the expertise that you've gained and put it to good use. All these efforts – together with the relationships you've established with decision-makers – can help get you the result you want. Yet this is not the end of the story.

Even when your proposed solution becomes law – or an administrative decision is taken – some citizen lobbying may still be needed. Indeed, reaching Step 10 is no guarantee of success. You will still have to make sure it is actually implemented. Should something go wrong, you must be ready to engage with the decision-makers and the whole administration. A new policy may never be enforced, or could be rapidly withdrawn by the same public authorities who supported it – or indeed by a new government. This occurred in Denmark when, after years of citizen campaigning for a fat tax (a price increase on unhealthy foods), it was scrapped just one year after being introduced.[53] Under these circumstances, you need to be alert and ready to go back to your lobbying toolbox to identify new courses of action. You must fight for your earlier success and resist any watering-down of the measure.

By this point, you might already have a group of citizens and perhaps organisations that support your action. Make sure you keep them informed and ready for action.

STEP 10: Stick to the (Lobbying) Rules

During your lobbying efforts, you must keep an eye on the law. What can and can't you do?

The good news is that as a citizen, you can lobby any public official. In general, each of us – whether a citizen or a permanent resident – enjoys the right to lobby our elected representatives. You don't have to qualify, sit an exam or face any major obstacles when you choose to speak out. Nor do you have to hire someone to do it for you. However, those who lobby for a third person, and are paid for it, are generally subject to 'professional lobbying' regulations. You, as a citizen, are generally exempt from these provisions insofar as what you are doing is not your job!

Furthermore, the sky is the limit when it comes to your citizen lobbying efforts. There are no restrictions on the number of emails, tweets or letters that you, as a citizen, can write, nor the number of websites and people you may bring on board, nor the phone calls you can make.

However, this is not to suggest that you have entirely free rein to lobby in the way you want. Unfortunately, you don't, and a few rules must be observed.

Firstly, be aware that excessive activity may qualify as stalking and harassment in your jurisdiction.

Secondly, some of the lobbying avenues you may decide to pursue might insist you comply with some procedural requirements. For example, you can't go to court without the assistance of a lawyer (see Step 4, The Judicial Avenue, page 196) or file an administrative complaint without following the (generally easy) pre-determined procedures (see page 191).

Thirdly, rules exist that, although they are predominantly aimed at professional lobbyists, may also apply to you. These rules apply to anyone seeking to influence decision-makers, regardless of whether they are paid or not for doing so. For instance, several countries limit the gifts you may offer to elected representatives and career officials. Their declared objective is to prevent public officials being tempted to capitalise on their status and power and, in some extreme circumstances, even engage in bribery.

Fourthly, while you as a citizen lobbyist can act alone – as many individuals from our illustrations do – you can also decide to team up with other citizens, start a movement, establish an organisation or even recruit a coalition of actors in order to build a critical mass. While this may enable you to gain as much support as possible, it can also bring your action under the professional lobbying rules. If you team up with an NPO and/or a company, your actions will become subject to those regulations.

Any lobbying effort designed to influence policymaking by mobilising the general public to support (or oppose) a particular initiative is generally known as grassroots lobbying. It has the advantage of making an issue more visible and educating the public about its relevance. Most citizen lobbying qualifies as grassroots advocacy, insofar as a citizen initiates it and others join in. While grassroots advocacy can be a 'weapon of the weak', by allowing new groups to gain a voice in the decisions affecting their lives, it can also be orchestrated and sponsored by industry. This phenomenon is called astro-turfing.[54] It mobilises the skills of professional lobbyists to help build an infrastructure for genuine activism. In other words, it is becoming increasingly common for companies to pay citizens to lobby for their cause. It sounds cynical to say so – but a lot of public activism, even if it looks like citizen lobbying, is organised behind the scenes by professional lobbyists.

Most importantly, be aware that lobbying is a constitutionally protected activity across the world. In other words, a sort of 'right to lobby' exists. This is because lobbying represents both freedom of speech and expression, as well as the right to petition the government. Virtually all liberal democracies recognise these fundamental rights – although to different extents.

The concept of petitioning the government dates back to the Magna Carta, a document which was signed by King John I in England in 1215. It reads:

> If we, our chief justice, our officials, or any of our servants
> offend in any respect against any man, or transgress any of
> the articles of the peace or of this security, and the offence
> is made known to four of the said twenty-five barons, they
> shall come to us – or in our absence from the kingdom to
> the chief justice—to declare it and claim immediate redress.

Although the power was only granted to the 25 barons elected by the King, they had the authority to petition him if they felt injustices were being imposed. Later, this right to petition was confirmed and extended by the 1689 Bill of Rights, which states that the King's subjects are entitled to petition him without fear of prosecution.

Drawing on these documents, the framers of the US Constitution added the Bill of Rights to their Constitution in 1789. It contained ten Amendments – the first of which was written by James Madison, and contained a clause recognising the right to petition government.

The right to petition our own governments – though often overlooked in comparison with other constitutional freedoms – is a major, foundational right recognised across liberal democracies. It grants people not only the freedom to stand up and speak out against injustices they feel are occurring, but also grants the power to help change those injustices.

In the US, the right to petition is one of the fundamental freedoms of all Americans, and has been construed quite extensively by the Supreme Court.[55] In the case of Noerr, the Supreme Court affirmed that 'the whole concept of representation depends upon the ability of the people to make their wishes known to their representatives'.[56]

Under the petition section of the US's first amendment, commonly referred to as the Petition Clause, people have the right to appeal to government about policies that affect them, or about which they feel strongly. This freedom includes the right to gather signatures in support of a cause and to lobby legislative bodies. A simpler definition of the right to petition is the right to present requests to the government without punishment or reprisal.

Most European countries do not recognise a right to petition the government as an autonomous right, but they certainly see it as a form of protected political expression. The European Union, however, established the right to petition to give EU citizens and residents a simple way of contacting institutions with a request or complaint. This right is conferred by EU citizenship, which is automatically granted to all nationals of the EU member states. A petition must relate to a subject falling within the EU's sphere of activity and must concern the petitioner directly. If this is not the case, the complaint is declared ineligible. Should you stumble upon the latter scenario, you might want to identify other avenues of action available to you.

Unlike the US, most European countries and the EU itself do not regulate professional lobbying. It remains first and foremost an activity that serves the goals of participatory democracy, now set out in Article 11 of the Treaty of the EU. However, anyone who seeks to directly or indirectly influence the EU decision-making process is expected to declare it in the EU Transparency Register. Although I am not a professional lobbyist, I was encouraged to register because my citizen lobbying activity often brings me in contact with MEPs as well as European Commission officials. I encourage anyone engaging with EU institutions to do the same. Although voluntary,[57] a failure to register may prevent you from entering the EU's institutional building, putting your long-awaited face-to-face meeting in jeopardy.

In addition, the International Covenant on Civil and Political Rights recognises that: 'Everyone shall have the right to freedom of expression; this right shall include freedom to seek, receive and impart information and ideas of all kinds ...'

In the United States, the act of citizen petitioning has been particularly effective in bringing about positive change. During the civil rights movement, for example, the Supreme Court upheld the rights of several groups of individuals who were protesting against segregation at public institutions such as libraries and schools, and ruled that these citizens were perfectly entitled to express their rights under the petition clause.

More recently, the same rights have been upheld in situations involving environmental protests. Oceana, an international organisation dedicated to marine protection and preservation, recently joined over 100,000 citizens in signing a petition protesting against longline fishing in many parts of the Atlantic Ocean. Certain endangered species of sea mammals, turtles and birds had been caught and sometimes killed as a result of the practice. A federal judge went on to ban longline fishing in many areas in order to protect marine wildlife.

This example shows how lobbying allows interest groups to put forward their views on public decisions that may affect them. It can also improve the quality of decision-making by opening up channels for technical expertise to inform legislators and decision-makers.

Conclusions

'Never doubt that a small group of thoughtful,
committed citizens can change the world.
Indeed, it is the only thing that ever has.'
Margaret Mead

Becoming a citizen lobbyist is a powerful antidote to our growing feelings of powerlessness. But there is more to it than that. Breaking free of the habit of passivity gives you the chance to channel your talents into effective engagement. This feels like an awakening. It comes from the sudden realisation that so much of our physical and social space is the fruit of somebody else's efforts. As our daily digital excursions remind us, we are increasingly powerless by design. Rising income inequality is not, as a matter of fact, the inevitable result of impersonal forces such as globalisation or automation.[1] It stems from hundreds of social, financial, tax and trade policy measures that benefit the people with a direct line to government.

Over half of the money given to US presidential candidates in the 2016 campaign came from just 158 families.[2] And the demographics of these 158 families are strikingly similar: 50 of them are in the *Forbes* 400 list of America's wealthiest billionaires, and many of them even live in the same neighbourhoods. They are overwhelmingly older, male and white, in an electorate that is increasingly young, female and black, Asian or Latino. These 158 families donated a total of $176 million; 138 of them backed President Trump.

While other liberal democracies are not quite so polarised, the overall picture of a government dominated by special interests is borne out by systemic imbalances that weaken the voices of ordinary citizens.

As a citizen lobbyist, you are bound to experience this imbalance first-hand. Even if your issue is small, local and affects relatively few people, you will start to feel a sense of injustice – at first superficially, then more deeply. The experience will change you. You will see, engage with and live out this imbalance of power and social injustice. Your fear will be turned into outrage before your outrage will turn into hope.

You may come to realise that beneath your issue there are deeper dynamics which call for a greater commitment to social justice and citizen empowerment. In other words, the problem you initially cared about is only a symptom of a more serious pathology that deserves your attention.

Nobody will force you to step up your efforts, but acting as a citizen lobbyist – even if you do it only once – will give you a deeper world view than you had before. At a time of acute societal polarisation, you will reach out and listen to those with whom you disagree. By now you know what kind of difference you can make to society and how.

I have my own opinions about public policy and politics, but they are not what this book is about. Regardless of whether you are a conservative, a progressive, a libertarian or a communist, a green or a pirate, atheist or theist, activist or politically inactive, the purpose of this book is to make you into an effective citizen lobbyist. The more we engage as citizens with our elected representatives, and the more we force our systems of governance to answer to us, the better government works for everyone.

At a time of growing disenchantment with the democratic system, we have no choice but to transform mounting distrust into an active democratic virtue. That's exactly what citizen lobbying does. Acting as a corrective device for our representative democracies, it offers a form of criticism and monitoring that allows citizens, policymakers and businesses to work better, together. And it does so by leveraging citizens' expertise and imagination, empowering ourselves and boasting our happiness. By striving for equality, citizen lobbying helps society to heal itself.

Each of you will decide for yourself what to fight for, and once you have found something you care passionately about – whatever it is – you now have the tools, tactics and mindset to become an effective advocate for change. Please share your citizen lobbying stories. Tell me (and the world) how they go and, regardless of the final outcome, how much you have learned from them.

Will lobbying became a new hobby, like chess, gardening or reading? If you too become an ambassador for the citizen lobbying movement, perhaps we will live in a more engaged society – and probably a happier one.

And remember that none of the big leaps forward for society, such as universal suffrage and civil rights, have happened without citizens' involvement. For change to happen, people who are unhappy with the status quo have to grab the bull by the horns and win the battle. You don't have to be a celebrity to make it happen.

It is up to us – and up to you.

End Notes

Introduction

1. Throughout the book, we'll explore some of these opportunities in more depth.

2. Alberto Alemanno, 'Unpacking the Principle of Openness in EU Law: Transparency, Participation and Democracy', *European Law Review*, Vol. 39, pp. 72–90 (2014). Available at: https://ssrn.com/abstract=2303644

3. Cass Sunstein, *Infotopia: How Many Minds Produce Knowledge*, Oxford University Press (2006); Cass Sunstein, *Republic.com*, Princeton University Press (2001); Cass Sunstein, *#Republic: Divided Democracy in the Age of Social Media*, Princeton University Press (2017).

4. E. J. Wood, 'Problem-Based Learning: Exploiting Knowledge of How People Learn to Promote Effective Learning', in *Bioscience Education E-Journal*, Vol. 3. Available at: http://www.bioscience.heacademy.ac.uk/journal/vol3/beej-3-5.htm

5. Dahlia Remler, 'Are 90% of academic papers really never cited? Reviewing the literature on academic citations', London School of Economics, Impact Blog, 23 April 2014.

6. Roberto Stefan Foa and Yascha Mounk, 'The Danger of Deconsolidation: The Democratic Disconnect', *Journal of Democracy*, July 2016, Volume 27, Number 3.

7. For an excellent introduction, see Jan-Werner Müller, *What is Populism?*, Penn University Press (2016).

8. For an introduction to happiness studies, see Derek Bok, *The Politics of Happiness: What Government Can Learn from the New Research on Well-Being*, Harvard University Press (2011). Current research on well-being derives from two general perspectives: the hedonic approach, which focuses on happiness and defines well-being in terms of pleasure attainment and pain avoidance; and

the eudaimonic approach, which focuses on self-realisation and defines well-being in terms of the degree to which a person is fully functioning. These two views have given rise to different research streams and a body of knowledge that is in some areas divergent and in others complementary. To know more, see E. Deci and R. Ryan, 'Hedonia, eudaimonia, and well-being: An introduction', *Journal of Happiness Studies*, Vol. 9, Issue 1, pp. 1–11 (2008).

9. B. Frey and A. Stutzer, 'What can Economists learn from happiness research?', *Journal of Economic Literature*, 40:402–435.

10. A. Sen, *Development as Freedom*, Oxford University Press (2001).

11. C. Barker and B. Martin, 'Participation: The Happiness Connection', *Journal of Public Deliberation*, Vol. 7, Issue 1 (2011).

12. Susan Pinker, *The Village Effect: How Face-To-Face Contact Can Make Us Healthier and Happier*, Penguin Random House (2015); 'Immunology: The pursuit of happiness', *Nature*, 27 November 2013. Available at: http://www.nature.com/news/immunology-the-pursuit-of-happiness-1.14225

13. Arie W. Kruglanski et al., 'The Psychology of Radicalization and Deradicalization: How Significance Quest Impacts Violent Extremism', *Political Psychology*, Vol. 35, pp. 69–93 (2014) .

14. See, for example, Michael Edwards, *Small Change: Why Business Won't Save the World*, Berrett-Koehler Publishers (2010).

15. Paul Monaghan and Philip Monaghan, *Lobbying for Good: How Business Advocacy Can Accelerate the Delivery of a Sustainable Economy*, Greenleaf Publishing (2014), p. 15.

16. Manuel Arriaga, *Rebooting Democracy — A Citizen's Guide To Reinventing Politics*, Thistle Publishing (2013).

17. Edelman's polling of 'informed publics' found a three-to-one margin of support for increased government regulation of the energy, food and financial services sectors. See: http://www.edelman.com/insights/intellectual-property/2016-edelman-trust-barometer/executive-summary/

18. For an economic argument supporting this position, see Mariana Mazzuccato, *The Entrepreneurial State*, Anthem Press (2013).

19. UNHCR, 'Global Trends: Forced Displacement in 2015' (2016).

20. For a primer on the Fourth Industrial Revolution, see Klaus Schwab, 'The Fourth Industrial Revolution', World Economic Forum (2015). Available at: http://www3.weforum.org/docs/Media/KSC_4IR.pdf. In his view, this new revolution is characterised by a fusion of technologies that is blurring the lines between the physical, digital and biological spheres building on the Third.

21. D. Altman, 'Bringing Direct Democracy Back In: Toward a three dimensional measure of democracy', *Democratization*, Vol. 20, pp. 615–614 (2013); R.J. Dalton and S.A. Weldon, 'Public Images of political parties: A necessary evil?', *West European Politics*, Vol. 28, pp. 931–951 (2005); M. Dogan, 'Erosion of Confidence in Thirty European Democracies', *Comparative Sociology*, Vol. 4, pp. 11–53 (2005); B. Stevenson and J. Wolfers, 'Trust in public institutions over the business cycle', Discussion paper series // *Forschungsinstitut zur Zukunft der Arbeit*, No. 5570 (2011).

22. James Adams, 'Causes and Electoral Consequences of Party Policy Shifts in Multiparty Elections: Theoretical Results and Empirical Evidence', *Annual Review of Political Science*, Vol. 15, pp. 401–419 (2012).

23. Check the recently established organisation, Apolitical, whose mission is to celebrate 'the men and women in government who are on the front lines of our greatest challenges'. See: www.apolitical.com

24. David Sarokin and Jay Schulkin, *Missed Information: Better Information for Building a Wealthier, More Suistainable Future*, The MIT Press (2016).

25. Manuel Castells, *Networks of Outrage and Hope: Social Movements in the Internet Age*, Polity (2015).

26. Clay Shirky, *Here Comes Everybody: The Power of Organising Without Organisations*, London: Penguin (2008).

27. Micah Sifry, *The Big Disconnect: Why the Internet Hasn't Changed Politics (Yet)*, OR Books (2014).

28. Philippe Aghion, Ufuk Akcigit, Antonin Bergeaud, Richard Blundell and David Hemous, 'Innovation, Income Inequality and Social Mobility', *VoxEU*, 28 July 2015.

29. Sergey Filippov, 'Government of the Future: How Digital Technology Will Change the Way We Live, Work and Government', *European Digital Forum Digital Insight*, The Lisbon Council and Nesta (2015).

30. See Jamie Bartlett and Heather Grabbe, 'E-democracy in the EU: the opportunities for digital politics to re-engage voters and the risks of disappointment', *Demos*, p. 8 (2015).

31. Alina Mungiu-Pippidi, 'Learning from Virtuous Circles', *Journal of Democracy*, Vol. 27, p. 96, p. 198 (2016).

32. Lee Drutman, *The Business of America is Lobbying: How Corporations Became Politicized and Politics Became More Corporate*, Oxford University Press (2015).

33. For an OECD perspective, see Alberto Alemanno, 'Stakeholder Engagement in Regulatory Policy', *OECD Regulatory Policy Outlook*, OECD Publishing (2015). Available at: https://ssrn.com/abstract=2701675. For a US perspective, see Matt Grossmann, *The Not-So-Special Interests: Interest Groups, Public Representation, and American Governance*, Stanford University Press (2012).

34. Kyle Peterson and Marc Pfitzer, 'Lobbying for Good', *Stanford Social Innovation Review* (2009).

35. Michael Edwards, *Civil Society*, Polity Press (2014), p. 46; Mary-Hunter McDonnell, 'Radical Repertoires: The Incidence and Impact of Corporate-Sponsored Social Activism', *Organization Science*, Vol. 27 (2016).

36. The Good Lobby website is available at: www.thegoodlobby.eu

Part I – The Problem

1. For a compelling account on the cognitive psychology of powerlessness, see Sendil Mullainathan and Eldar Shafir, *Scarcity: Why having too little means so much*, Henry Holt (2013).

2. Ibid.

3. When people are in the presence of others, they are less likely to offer help than when they are alone. This reinforces inaction.

4. Brian Stipelman, *That Broader Definition of Liberty: The Theory and Practice of the New Deal*, Lexington (2012), p. 243.

5. John Thorley, *Athenian Democracy*, Routledge (2004).

6. James Stuart Mill, *Considerations on Representative Government (1861)*, The Floating Press, May 1, 2009.

7. For one of the best defenses of liberal democracies, see, Karl Popper, *The Open Society and Its Enemies*, Princeton University Press (2013).

8. James Madison, *Federalist papers*, no. 10, New York Packet, November 23, (1787).

9. Robert Dahl, *Democracy and its Critics*, Yale University Press (1989).

10. David Van Reybrouck, 'Why Elections Are Bad for Democracy', *Guardian*, 29 June 2016.

11. Joseph Schumpeter, *Capitalism, Socialism and Democracy*, Routledge (2003), p. 269.

12. Jean-Jacques Rousseau, *Du Contrat Social*, Chapter XV.

13. James Stuart Mill, *Considerations on Representative Government (1861)*, The Floating Press, May 1, 2009, p. 204.

14. Christopher H. Ache and Larry M. Bartels, *Democracy for Realists: Why Elections Do Not Produce Responsive Government*, Princeton University Press (2016).

15. Markus Prior, *Post-Broadcast Democracy: How Media Choice Increase Inequalities in Political Involvement and Polarized Elections*, Cambridge University Press (2007).

16. For a masterful account of how citizens exercise power alongside and beyond the ballot box, see Pierre Rosanvallon, *Counter-Democracy: Politics in an Age of Distrust*, Cambridge University Press (2008).

17. *Massive Millennial Poll*, a survey of attitudes about sex, politics, tech, culture and more in 2015.

18. The Hansard Society's Audit of Political Engagement, 2016.

19. 'Voters can't name their MEPs as poll highlights disengagement with EU', *Guardian*, 10 May 2014.

20. Martin Gillens et al., 'Testing theories of American politics: elites, interest groups, and average citizens', *Perspectives on Politics*. Vol. 12, pp. 564–581 (2014); Martin Gillens, *Affluence and Influence:*

Economic Inequality and Political Power in America, Princeton University Press (2010).

21. Thomas Ferguson, *Golden Rule: The Investment Theory of Party Competition and the Logic of Money-Driven Political Systems*, University of Chicago Press (1995).

22. 'An Economy for the 99%: It's time to build a human economy that benefits everyone, not just the privileged few', Oxfam Briefing Paper (2017). Oxfam's calculations use the wealth of the richest individuals from *Forbes*' billionaires list and the wealth of the bottom 50 per cent from the Credit Suisse Global Wealth Databook 2016.

23. 'An Economy for the 1%, How privilege and power in the economy drive extreme inequality and how this can be stopped', 210 Oxfam Briefing Paper (2016).

24. The material on page(s) 1, from '62 people own same as half world – Oxfam,' 2016 is reproduced with the permission of Oxfam, Oxfam House, John Smith Drive, Cowley, Oxford OX4 2JY, UK www.oxfam .org.uk. Oxfam does not necessarily endorse any text or activities that accompany the materials.

25. Considerable empirical work finds that there is no consistent correlation between money spent on outcomes in any given case.

26. Center for Responsive Politics, lobbying database available at: https://www.opensecrets.org/lobby/

27. Lobbyingfacts.eu, 'List of biggest NGO spenders on EU lobbying reveals register's absurd data', November 12, 2015. Available at: https://lobbyfacts.eu/articles/12-11-2015/list-biggest-ngo-spenders -eu-lobbying-reveals-register%E2%80%99s-absurd-data

28. See '7,000 and counting – Lobbying meetings of the European Commission', Transparency International (2015)

29. For an OECD perspective, see Alberto Alemanno, 'Stakeholder Engagement in Regulatory Policy', *OECD Regulatory Policy Outlook*, OECD Publishing (2015). Available at: https://ssrn.com/ abstract=2701675. For a US perspective, see Matt Grossmann, *The Not-So-Special Interests: Interest Groups, Public Representation, and American Governance*, Stanford University Press (2012).

30. Cass Sunstein, *Infotopia: How Many Minds Produce Knowledge*, Oxford University Press (2006); Cass Sunstein, *Republic.com*, Princeton University Press (2001); Cass Sunstein, *Republic: Divided Democracy in the Age of Social Media*, Princeton University Press (2017).

31. APSA Task Force on Inequality and American Democracy (2004), p. 651.

32. Clay Shirky, 'The Political Power of Social Media: Technology, the Public Sphere, and Political Change', *Foreign Affairs*, Vol. 90, No. 1, pp. 28–41 (January/February 2011).

33. Colin Crouch, *Post-Democracy*, Polity Press (2004).

34. William D. Nordhaus, Paul Samuelson and Global Public Goods, 'A commemorative essay for Paul Samuelson', Yale University (May 5, 2005).

35. Roberto Stefan Foa and Yascha Mounk, 'The Danger of Deconsolidation: The Democratic Disconnect', *Journal of Democracy*, Vol. 27, Number 3, (July 2016).

36. 'Youth Voter Participation: Involving Today's Young in Tomorrow's Democracy' *IDEA* (1999).

37. James Madison, *Federalist papers*, no. 10, New York Packet (November 23, 1787).

38. Alexis de Tocqueville, *Democracy in America* (1824).

39. Robert Dahl, *Who Governs*, Yale University Press (1961).

40. Donald C. Pennington, *The Social Psychology of Behaviour in Small Groups*, Psychology Press (2002).

41. See, for example, Jefferson and Rush quoted from The People's Bicentennial Commission, *Voices of the American Revolution*, Bantam Books (1974), pp. 175–76.

42. James Russell Lowell, 'The Place of the Independent in Politics', *Political Essays*, New York, 13 April, 1888.

43. John Dewey, 'Democracy and Education', *An Introduction to the Philosophy of Education*, Macmillan (1916).

44. Lija Farnham, Gihani Fernando, Mike Perigo and Colleen Brosman, with Paul Tough, 'Rethinking How Students Succeed', *Stanford Social Innovation Review* (February 2015).

45. Richard Howell Allen, *Impact Teaching*, Allyn and Bacon (2002).

46. Ken Robinson and Lou Aronica, *Creative Schools: The Grassroots Revolution That's Transforming Education*, Viking (2015).

47. The Value of Extracurricular Activities Infographic: http://elearning infographics.com/value-extracurricular-activities-infographic/

48. The Impact of Extracurricular Activity on Student Academic Performance, University of California, Sacramento, available at: http://www.csus.edu/oir/research%20projects/student%20activity%20report%202009.pdf

49. B Schwarz, *The Paradox of Choice: Why More is Less*, Harper Perennial (2004); Renata Salecl, *Choice*, Profile Books (2010).

50. Daniel Kahneman and Amos Twersky, *Judgment Under Uncertainty: Heuristics and Biases*, 185 Science (4157), 1124 *et seq.* (1974).

51. For a fascinating account of the genesis of applied behavioural sciences, see Daniel Kahneman, *Thinking Fast and Slow*, FSG (2001).

52. At the time of publication of this book, the members of the Eurozone are: Austria, Belgium, Cyprus, Estonia, Finland, France, Germany, Greece, Ireland, Italy, Latvia, Lithuania, Luxembourg, Malta, The Netherlands, Portugal, Slovakia, Slovenia and Spain.

53. Eric J. Johnson and Daniel Goldstein, 'Do Defaults Save Lives?', *Science*, Vol. 21, pp. 1338–1339 (Nov 2003).

54. See, for example, Suzanne Higgs and Jason Thomas, 'Social Influence and Eating', *Current Opinion in Behavioral Sciences*, Vol. 9, pp. 1–6 (June 2016); T. Cruwys, K.E. Bevelander and R.C. Hermans, 'Social modeling of eating: a review of when and why social influence affects food intake and choice', *Appetite*, Vol. 86, pp. 3–18 (2015).

55. To know the genesis of this research, see Daniel Kahneman, *Thinking, Fast and Slow*, Farrar, Straus and Giroux (2011).

56. Dan Ariely, writing in response to an online Q&A on Quora, 20 November 2016: quora.com/session/Dan-Ariely/1

57. Gerard Hastings, *The Marketing Matrix: How the corporation gets its power – and how we can reclaim it*, Routledge (2012).

58. Charles Duhigg, 'How Companies Learn Your Secrets', *New York Times*, Feb. 16, 2012.

59. For an introduction to Big Data, see Viktor Mayer-Schönberger and Kenneth Cukier, *Big Data: A Revolution That Will Transform How We Live, Work, and Think,* John Murray (2013).

60. Adam D. I. Kramer, Jamie E. Guillory and Jeffrey T. Hancock, 'Experimental evidence of massive-scale emotional contagion through social network', *PNAS*, Vol. 111 (24) pp. 8788–8790 (2014).

61. Robert M. Bond et al., 'A 61-million-person experiment in social influence and political mobilization', *Nature*, Vol. 489 (13 September 2012).

62. Immanuel Kant, *Kant's Principles of Politics, including his essay on Perpetual Peace. A Contribution to Political Science*, trans. W. Hastie, Clark (1891).

63. Ibid.

64. Jennifer Stark and Nicholas Diakopoulos, 'Uber seems to offer better service in areas with more white people. That raises some tough questions', *Washington Post*, March 10, 2016.

65. Ibid.

66. Frank Pasquale, *The Black Box Society: The Secret Algorithms that Control Money and Information*, Harvard University Press (2015).

67. To know more, check the MIT Affect Computing Research group at: http://affect.media.mit.edu/projects.php

68. 'Tesco's In-Store Ads Watch You – and It Looks Like You Need Coffee', *Businessweek.com*, 4 November 2014; Kevin Rawlinson, 'Facial recognition technology: How well does it work?', 3 February 2015.

69. Yohei Kawaguchi et al., 'Face Recognition-based Lecture Attendance System': http://www.mm.media.kyoto-u.ac.jp/old/research/doc/682/FRLASinAEARU.pdf. See also 'Chinese lecturer to use facial-recognition technology to check boredom levels among his students', *The Telegram*, 12 September 2016.

70. Richard Fording and Sanford Schram, 'The Cognitive and Emotional Sources of Trump Support: The Case of Low-Information Voters', unpublished paper mentioned in Richard Fording and Sanford Schram, 'Low information voters are a crucial part of Trump's support', *Washington Post*, November 7, 2016.

71. It claimed publicly to have 5,000 data points on each of the 200 million voters in the 2016 US elections.

72. Sendil Mullainathan and Eldar Shafir, *Scarcity: Why having too little means so much*, Henry Holt (2013).

Part II – The Solution

1. Fran Peavey, *Heart Politics*, New Society Publishers (1986), p. 176.

2. Albert Hirschman, *Exit Voice and Loyalty*, Harvard University Press (1970). According to his theory, in any form of relationship, we have essentially two possible responses when we perceive a decrease in quality or benefit to us: we can exit (withdraw from the relationship); or, we can voice (attempt to repair or improve the relationship through communication of the complaint, grievance or proposal for change).

3. The *Economist* Intelligence Unit, 'Motivated by impact: A new generation seek to make their mark', 21 July 2016.

4. The amount of lobbying efforts by the corporate world is truly unprecedented. In the US, the $2.6 billion in reported corporate lobbying spending is now more than the combined under $2 billion budget for the entire Senate ($860 million) and the entire House ($1.18 billion). In the EU, business accounts for roughly 90 per cent of all reported lobbying expenditures in the EU. See '7,000 and counting – Lobbying meetings of the European Commission', *Transparency International* (2015).

5. Ibid.

6. Ibid.

7. Eric Lipton and Brooke Williams, 'How Think Tanks Amplify Corporate America's Influence', *New York Times*, August 7, 2016.

8. Charlemagne, 'The dodgy side of Brussels think-tanks', *Economist*, 17 August 2009.

9. For a study of UK and German think tanks, see Hartwig Pautz, *Think-Tanks, Social Democracy and Social Policy*, Palgrave Macmillan (2012).

10. The US has more think tanks than the next nine countries world-wide combined. See Jesper Dahl Kelstrup, *The Politics of Think Tanks in Europe*, Routledge (2016).

11. Ibid.

12. Naomi Oreskes and Eric Conway, *Merchants of Doubt*, Bloomsbury (2010).

13. The legal systems govern lobbying only insofar as it qualifies as professional lobbying, i.e. a service provided by a third party against remuneration.

14. James Madison, *Federalist papers*, no. 63, New York Packet, November 23, 1787.

15. See Reno v. ACLU, U.S. 521 (1997).

16. For a sober analysis of the actual role of the internet in democratising our society, see Micah Sifry, *The Big Disconnect: Why the Internet Hasn't Changed Politics (Yet)*, OR Books (2014).

17. See Lynn Sanders, 'Against Deliberation', *Political Theory*, Vol. 25, n. 3 (June 1997).

18. Rumely v. United States, 197 F.2d 166, 173–174, 177 (D.C. Cir. 1952).

19. Alberto Alemanno, 'Stakeholder Engagement in Regulatory Policy', *Regulatory Policy Outlook*, OECD Publishing (2015).

20. See, for example, J. Dryzek, *Deliberative Democracy and Beyond: Liberals, Critics, Contestations*, Oxford University Press (2000).

21. Rowe and Frewer, 'A Typology of Public Engagement Mechanisms', *Science, Technology, & Human Values*, Vol. 30, Issue 2, pp. 251–290 (2016).

22. OECD, Indicators of Regulatory Management Systems, Regulatory Policy Committee, 2009 Report.

23. Adam Grant, *Originals: How Non-Conformists Move the World*, Penguin Random House (2016).

24. Cynthia R. Farina and Mary J. Newhart, 'Rulemaking 2.0: Understanding and Getting Better Public Participation', Cornell Law School (2013). Available at: http://scholarship.law.cornell.edu/cgi/viewcontent.cgi?article=1014&context=ceri

25. Chris Welzel and Russel Dalton, *The Civic Culture Transformed*:

From Allegiant to Assertive Citizens, Cambridge University Press (2015).

26. For a theory of the public sphere, Michael Edwards, *Civil Society*, Polity Press, 2014, p. 66 ss, 115.

27. Antonio R. Damasio, *Descartes' error: emotion, reason, and the human brain*, Penguin (1995).

28. Dacher Keltner, *The Power Paradox*, Allen Lane (2016), p. 22.

29. Manuel Castells, *Communication Power*, Oxford University Press (2009).

30. This is self-government by citizens as opposed to representative government in the name of the citizens. Benjamin Barber, *Strong Democracy: Participatory Politics for a New Age*, University of California Press (1984).

31. C. Cohen and J. Kahne, *Participatory Politics: New Media and Youth Political Action*, MacArthur Foundation Youth and Participatory Politics Research Networks (June 2012).

32. Michael Edwards, *Civil Society*, Polity Press (2014,) p. 122.

33. Robert D. Putnam, *Bowling Alone: The Collapse and Revival of American Community*, Simon & Schuster (2000).

34. See, for example, C. Pateman, *Participation and Democratic Theory*, Cambridge University Press (1970).

35. Micah Sifry, *The Big Disconnect: Why the Internet Hasn't Changed Politics (Yet)*, OR Books (2014), p. 150.

36. Christopher H. Achen and Larry M. Bartels, *Democracy for Realists: Why Elections Do Not Produce Responsive Government*, Princeton (2016), p. 19.

37. See Jamie Bartlett and Heather Grabbe, *E-democracy in the EU: the opportunities for digital politics to re-engage voters and the risks of disappointment*, Demos (2016), p. 8.; Heather Grabbe and Stefan Lehne, *Emotional Intelligence for EU Democracy*, Carnegie Europe (2015).

38. Christopher H. Achen and Larry M. Bartels, *Democracy for Realists: Why Elections Do Not Produce Responsive Government*, Princeton (2016).

39. James Madison, *Federalist papers*, no. 63, New York Packet, November 23, 1787.

40. Sherman J. Clark, 'A Populist Critique of Direct Democracy', *Harvard Law Review*, 112(2):434 (December 1988).

41. J. Bourgon, 'Responsive, Responsible and Respected Government: Toward a New Public Administration Theory', *International Review of Administrative Sciences*, Vol. 73, pp. 7–26 (2016).

42. Jason Stanley, *How Propaganda Works*, Princeton (2015), p. 7.

Part III – The Toolbox

1. OECD, 'Government at a Glance 2013', OECD Publishing, p. 19.

2. Reeve Bull, *Making the Administrative State 'Safe for Democracy': A Theoretical and Practical Analysis of Citizen Participation in Agency Decisionmaking*, ACUS, pp. 11–13 (2013).

3. David Lowery and Virginia Grey, 'A neopluralist perspective on research on organized interests', *Political Research Quarterly*, Vol. 57, pp. 163–75 (2004).

4. Revolving Doors, Corporate Europe Observatory, available at: http://corporateeurope.org/power-lobbies/revolving-doors

5. www.startupticker.ch/en/news/may-2016/another-ambitious-privacy-start-up-with-headquarter-in-switzerland

6. On data protection advocacy, see: https://iapp.org/news/a/an-advocacy-storm-is-coming-could-it-water-your-garden/

7. Andrew Pollack, 'Drug Goes From $13.50 a Tablet to $750, Overnight', *New York Times*, September 20, 2015.

8. Alan Webber, 'What's So New About the New Economy?', *Harvard Business Review* Jan–Feb. 1993; William Isaacs, 'Dialogue: The Art Of Thinking Together', September 14, 1999.

9. Kyle Peterson, Marc Pfitzer, 'Lobbying for good', *Stanford Social Innovation Review* (Winter 2009).

10. For an overview of behavioural informed regulation, see Alberto Alemanno and Alessandro Spina, 'Nudging Legally – On Checks

and Balances of Behavioral Regulation', *International Journal of Constitutional Law*, Vol. 12, Issue 2 (2014).

11. RCTs are specific experiments, widely used in the medical field, in which the efficacy of an intervention is studied by comparing the effects of the intervention on a study population, which is randomly allocated in different subgroups. The subgroups are exposed to a differential course of treatment: one of them – the control group – is not treated (or receives a 'placebo'), whilst the other subgroup – the intervention group – is exposed to the treatment. The impact of the intervention is then measured by comparing the results in both subgroups.

12. David Krackhardt and Jeffrey R. Hanson, 'Informal Networks: The Company Behind the Chart', *Harvard Business Review* (July–August 1993).

13. Jan Beyers, 'Voice and Access: Political Practices of European Interest Associations', *European Union Politics*, Vol. 5, Issue 2, pp. 211–240 (2004).

14. For an introduction to the US system, Craig Holman, 'The Structure and Organisation of Congress and the Practice of Lobbying', *The Lobbying Manual*, ABA 2009, p. 585. For an introduction to the EU system, watch 'Understanding Europe: Why it Matters and What it Can Offer You', available on Coursera.

15. R. Parker and A. Alemanno, 'Towards Effective Regulatory Cooperation Under TTIP: A Comparative Overview of the EU and US Legislative and Regulatory Systems', European Commission, Brussels (May 2014).

16. Article 11(3) Treaty on the Functioning of the European Union.

17. New Zealand Parliament, Parliament Brief: Select Committees, How Parliament Work Fact Sheets, available at: www.parliament.nz

18. *Sociaal-Economische Raad* (2013), *Energieakkoord voor duurzame groei*, available at: http://www.ser.nl/nl/publicaties/overige/2010-2019/2013/energieakkoord-duurzame-groei.aspx

19. The commitment to assess the scope for further action to strengthen the protection of whistle-blowers in EU law was affirmed by President

Juncker in the Letter of Intent complementing his 2016 State of the Union speech and in the 2017 Commission Work Programme.

20. See, Bruno Frey et al., 'Direct Democracy and the Constitution', in A. Marciano (ed.), 'Constitutional Mythologies: New Perspectives on Controlling the State', *Studies in Public Choice*, Vol. 23 (2011), and, for a EU perspective, Alberto Alemanno, 'Unpacking the Principle of Openness in EU Law – Transparency, Participation and Democracy', *European Law Review* (2014).

21. Charles Blankart, '*Bewirken Referenden und Volksinitiativen einen Unterschied in der Politik?*' *Staatwissenschaften und Staatspraxis*, Vol. 3, pp. 509–524; Matt Qvortrup, 'Power to the People! But How? The Different Uses of Referendums Around the World', *Political Studies Review* (2014).

22. Victor Cuesta-Lopez, 'A Comparative Approach to the Regulation on the European Citizens' Initiative', *Perspectives on European Politics and Society*, Vol. 13, Issue 3,pp. 257–269 (2011).

23. For an overview, see Nancy Roberts and Raymond Trevor Bradley, 'Stakeholder Collaboration and Innovation: A Study of Public Policy Initiation at the State Level', *Journal of Applied Behavioural Sciences*, Vol. 27, pp. 209–227 (1991).

24. OECD, Regulatory Policy in Perspective, p. 124.

25. For more information and guidelines, see the Petitions Web Portal of the European Parliament: https://petiport.secure.europarl.europa.eu//petitions/en/main

26. For more information, see: https://petition.parliament.uk/help

27. Koussouris Sotirios, Yannis Charalabidis and Dimitrios Askounis 'A review of the European Union eParticipation action pilot projects', *Transforming Government: People, Process and Policy*, Vol. 5, pp. 8–19 (2011).

28. For an account of the FOIA movement from one of its leaders, see Helen Darbishire, 'A Right Emerges: The History of the Right of Access to Information and Its Link with Freedom of Expression', in Peter Molnar, *Free Speech and Censorship around the World*, CEU Press (2014).

29. See the webpage of Right2INFO.org for an up-to-date presentation of good law and practice that could be helpful to advocates seeking to promote the right to information. Sweden's Freedom of the Press Act of 1766 is the oldest in the world.

30. United States Supreme Court in NLRB v. Robbins Tire Co. 437 U.S. 214, 242 (1978).

31. David Babbs, 'Forest sell-off U-turn is a victory for people power', *Guardian*, 17 February 2011.

32. Henry Jenkins et al., *By Any Media Necessary – The New Youth Activism*, NYU (2016).

33. Corey Binns, 'Civil Rights Goes Digital', *Stanford Social Innovation Review* (Winter 2016), pp. 15–16.

34. Henry Jenkins, *Convergence Culture: Where Old and New Media Collide*, NYU Press (2006).

35. Emma Howard, 'How "clicktivism" has changed the face of political campaigns', *Guardian*, 24 September 2014.

36. For a critique of 'clickactivism', see Stuart Shulman, 'The Case Against Mass E-mails: Perverse Incentives and low Quality Public Participation in U.S. Federal Rulemaking', *Policy & Internet*, Vol. 1, pp. 23–53 (2009). For a response, see David Karpf, 'Online Political Mobilization from the Advocacy Group's Perspective: Looking Beyond Clicktivism', Vol. 2: Iss. 4, Article 2 (2010).

37. Communication from the Commission on the European Citizens' Initiative 'Water and sanitation are a human right! Water is a public good, not a commodity!', Brussels, 19.3.2014 COM(2014) 177 final.

38. Duncan Matthews, 'The Rise and Fall of the Anti-Counterfeiting Trade Agreement (ACTA): Lessons for the European Union', Queen Mary School of Law Legal Studies, Research Paper No. 127/2012. Available at: SSRN: https://ssrn.com/abstract=2161764

39. Danah Boyd, *It's Complicated: The Social Lives of Networked Teens*, Yale University Press (2014).

40. Kyle Peterson and Marc Pfitzer, 'Lobbying for Good', *Stanford Social Innovation Review* (Winter 2009).

41. Ibid.

42. Mary-Hunter McDonnell, 'Radical Repertoires: The Incidence and Impact of Corporate-Sponsored Social Activism', *Organization Science*, Vol. 27 (2016).

43. Ibid.

44. The Taproot Foundation is a 501 non-profit organisation that engages design, marketing, IT, strategic management and human resources professionals in pro bono service projects to build the infrastructure of other non-profit organisations. Its global pro directory is available at: https://www.taprootfoundation.org/about -probono/global-pro-bono

45. Vanessa Chase Lockshin, *The Storytelling Non-Profit – A practical guide to telling stories that raise money and awareness*, Lockshin Consulting Inc (2016).

46. Nathalie Kylander and Christopher Stone, 'The Role of Brand in the Nonprofit Sector', *Stanford Social Innovation Review* (Spring 2012).

47. If you would like to learn more about non-profit storytelling: Julie Dixon, 'Building a Storytelling Culture', *Stanford Social Innovation Review*, 27 October 2014.

48. Walter Lippman, *Public Opinion*, Harcourt, Brace and Company (1922).

49. George Monbiot, *An Activist's Guide to Exploiting the Media*, Bookmarks (2001).

50. Lina Srivastava, 'About and Basic Framework, Transmedia Activism', available at: www.transmedia-activism.com

51. The concept of Disco Soup started in Germany, when young people were cooking a 'protest soup' for a demonstration against agro-industrial practices.

52. Annie McKee, 'Empathy Is Key to a Great Meeting', *Harvard Business Review* (March 23 2015).

53. 'Denmark's food taxes, A fat chance', *Economist*, 12 November 2012

54. Edward T. Walker, *Grassroots for Hire, Public Affairs Consultants in American Democracy*, Cambridge University Press (2014).

55. Contrary to popular opinion, the Supreme Court has not yet resolved whether lobbying is constitutionally protected. Belying this fact, courts, Congress and scholars mistakenly assume that lobbying

is protected under the Petition Clause. Because scholars have shared the mistaken assumption that the Petition Clause protects the practice of 'lobbying', no research to date has looked closely at the Petition Clause doctrine and the history of petitioning in relation to lobbying. In a recent opinion addressing petitioning in another context, the Supreme Court unearthed the long history behind the right to petition and argued for the importance of this history for future interpretation of the Petition Clause. See Maggie McKinley, 'Lobbying and the Petition Clause', *Stanford Law Review*, Vol. 68, 1131 (2016).

56. Eastern Railroad Presidents Conference v Noerr Motor Freight Inc, 365 US 127 (1961).

57. The register has grown at a rate of around 1,000 a year, to reach over 10,000 organisations today. It is estimated that the actual coverage of the register is 60–75 per cent of lobbying organisations active at EU level.

Conclusions

1. As recently argued, 'economic trends are not acts of God'. Thomas Piketty, *Capital in the Twenty-First Century*, Harvard University Press (2014).

2. 'Buying power', Investigation by the *New York Times*, October 15, 2015.

Resources for Citizen Lobbyists

Here some resources no citizen lobbyist should do without.

Online petition resources
38 Degrees (38degrees.org.uk)
Founded in the UK by a group of campaigners who were 'determined to do something different', 38 Degrees currently has 3 million members. As well as hosting petitions on its website, the group prides itself on holding MPs to account by actively pressuring them both in person and online.

Avaaz (Avaaz.org)
Avaaz is the largest activist site in the world, and takes its name from the Farsi word for 'voice'. Operating in seventeen different languages, the platform counts over 41 million members who have signed at least one of its many petitions. Topics range from human rights abuses in Burma and FGM in Somalia, to war in Syria and African elephant poaching.

Causes (causes.com)
Best-known as a fundraising tool, this site provides some basic petition and pledging functions. Causes is integrated with Facebook and therefore easy for its users to pass on, which is a useful feature for those with active audiences there.

Change (change.org)

This popular and simple tool allows you to create a petition for free, but charges a fee for exporting or downloading the final list. It does have a sizeable, active community, which makes it an attractive option if you want more reach.

Clicksign (clicksign.com)

An online service that ensures petition signatures are authentic and safe. It also allows for monitoring of the signing processes and provides a secure vault to keep documents safe.

Moveon (petitions.moveon.org)

A US based website that aims to bring concerned citizens into contact with useful organisations and provide them with the tools to start their own grassroots campaign. Tools include online petitions and a network of over 8 million supporters, with a direct line to legislators.

The Petition Site (thepetitionsite.com)

One of the oldest online petition tools, this site run by Care2 offers free basic features which are similar to those available on Change.org, but charges fees to promote the petition or download names.

Petition2Congress (petition2congress.com)

A free US platform for citizens to post ideas and create petitions they can send directly to policy-makers on Capitol Hill.

SignOn (signon.org)
Recently developed by MoveOn.org, SignOn is still in the beta testing stage, but provides a simple, free petition tool that lets you download the list of names as a PDF file. This is useful when it comes to delivering the petition, but less so for a pledge.

WeMove (wemove.eu)
With nearly 500,000 members, WeMove is the new kid on the block. It aims to bridge the gap between European citizens and their representatives in Brussels by acting as a pan-European tool for linking together NGOs and online campaigning platforms.

Advocacy non-governmental organisations
The Action Network (www.actionnetwork.org)
A fully integrated online platform for activists and citizens alike to organise petitions, protests, events and much more so that they can build an entire movement using just one system.

Democracy 21 (democracy21.org)
Democracy 21 and its education arm work to eliminate the undue influence of big money in American politics. The organisation promotes campaign finance reform and other related political reforms to accomplish these goals.

GetUp! (getup.org.au)
An Australian progressive online activist platform. Its mission is to work towards a thriving democracy in Australia, where everyday people can have an impact in democracy.

ONE (one.org)

ONE is a campaigning and advocacy organisation of nearly 8 million people around the world taking action to end extreme poverty and preventable disease, particularly in Africa.

Rate Your Politician (thevoterssay.com)

An integrated online platform for citizens in the United States of America, Canada, Australia, England, Scotland and Wales to track the voting patterns of legislators, vote on their performance and post information about issues that concern them.

WITNESS (witness.org)

WITNESS is a human rights non-profit organisation based out of Brooklyn, New York. Its mission is to partner with on-the-ground organisations to support the documentation of human rights violations and their consequences, in order to further public engagement, policy change and justice.

Freedom of Information services

AsktheEU (asktheeu.org)

An online platform where citizens can request information directly from EU institutions.

The FOIA Machine (foiamachine.org)

The United States launched a new FOIA Hub, but the privately run FOIA Machine is still be more commonly used. Despite its initial ambition, the FOIA Machine does not yet allow you to file and track requests to governmental and public agencies worldwide.

FYI.org.nz
The FOI request service in New Zealand.

Right to Know (RighttoKnow.org.au)
An Australia based FOI request service.

WhatDoTheyKnow (whatdotheyknow.com)
A UK based FOI request service. Requests are made by users and published online for the public to see, thus making the need for multiple requests from different people unnecessary.

Crowdfunding
Crowdjustice (crowdjustice.org)
A platform, geared specifically towards legal cases, to help raise funds, gather support and increase public awareness.

StartSomeGood (startsomegood.com)
StartSomeGood is a crowdfunding platform exclusively for social change initiatives. They help social entrepreneurs, non-profits and community groups raise the funds they need to make a difference.

Legislative monitoring
Institutional sources
Australia
Australian parliament (aph.gov.au): a comprehensive website with various resources including details on current debates, voting records, speeches and petitions.

Canada

Canadian parliament (parl.canadiana.ca): provides records of speeches made in the Senate and House of Commons in both English and French.

European Union

Eur-lex (eur-lex.europa.eu): the official website of European Union law and other public documents of the EU. Published in the 24 languages of the EU.

France

National Assembly (assemblee-nationale.fr): website available in multiple languages, records are in French only.

Senate (www.senat.fr): website available in multiple languages, records are in French only.

Germany

National parliament (bundestag.de/en): website in available in multiple languages, records in German only.

New Zealand

New Zealand parliament (www.parliament.nz/en): access to Hansard records in both English and Maori.

New Zealand Gazette (gazette.govt.nz): the official journal of the New Zealand Government and constitutional record.

United Kingdom

Hansard (hansard.parliament.uk): a record of all speeches

delivered on the floors of the House of Commons and House of Lords.

The United Nations
UNBISNET (unbisnet.un.org): UNBISNET maintains a record of speeches, publications, resolutions, voting records and all other public documents.

United States
Congress (congress.gov): detailed information on current debates and bills under consideration.

The Library of Congress (loc.gov): tracks federal legislation in action.

Media outlets
International:
Al Jazeera: aljazeera.com
Economist: economist.com
Guardian: theguardian.com/international
Politico (both in the US and Europe): politico.com

Australia:
Canberra Times: canberratimes.com.au/federal-politics

Canada:
Globe and Mail: theglobeandmail.com/news/politics
National Post: news.nationalpost.com/category/news/
   canada/canadian-politics

European Union:
EU Observer: euobserver.com
Euractiv: euractiv.com
New Europe: neweurope.eu

France:
Mediapart: mediapart.fr/journal/france
Le Monde: lemonde.fr

Germany:
Cicero: cicero.de
Der Spiegel: spiegel.de (english) spiegel.de/international
Frankfurter Allgemeine Zeitung: faz.net
Süddeutsche Zeitung: sueddeutsche.de
Verfassungsblog: verfassungsblog.de

New Zealand:
NZ Herald: nzherald.co.nz/politics

United Kingdom:
Financial Times: ft.com
Guardian: theguardian.com
New Statesman: newstatesman.com
Spectator: spectator.co.uk
Telegraph: telegraph.co.uk

United States:
The Hill: thehill.com
Politifact: http://www.politifact.com

Real Clear Politics: realclearpolitics.com
Washington Post: washingtonpost.com

Pro bono legal services
International
International Bridges to Justice (ibj.org)
Based in Switzerland, IBJ has been developing and expanding its tools to support defenders of justice and human rights worldwide. Their global program is designed to reach the largest number of human rights and criminal justice defenders possible. They offer a wide range of training manuals, country assessment and scorecard tools, and other resources, all accessible to lawyers everywhere through their e-learning program.

PILnet (pilnet.org)
Established in 1997 as the Public Interest Law Initiative in Transitional Societies at Columbia University (PILI) to promote the use of law as a tool to serve the interests of the whole of society rather than those of a powerful few. They link lawyers from all across Europe with not-for-profit organisations (NPOs) in need of legal support.

European Union
The Good Lobby (thegoodlobby.eu)
Established in 2016, TGL is a skill-sharing community connecting academics and professionals to civil society organisations that need to receive their expertise. It democratises lobbying by offering pro bono advice while training a new generation of citizen lobbyists.

Australia

Australia Pro Bono Centre (probonocentre.org.au)
An independent centre of legal expertise, providing publications, surveys, conferences, directories and performance reports.

Czech Republic (Czechia)

Pro Bono Alliance (probonocentrum.cz)
A non-profit NGO of lawyers whose foremost goal is to achieve systematic changes in the Czech legal system in order to increase its effectiveness in protecting human rights, public interests and important common values.

France

AADH (aadh.fr)
The Alliance of Lawyers for Human Rights (*Alliance des Avocats pour les Droits de l'Homme*) is an association which coordinates the provision of free and confidential legal advice services for NGOs, associations and institutions dedicated to the protection of human rights, regardless of their national or international dimension.

Ireland

Public Interest Law Alliance (pila.ie)
PILA is an Irish hub of public interest law that supports lawyers, organisations, universities and students to help marginalised and disadvantaged people. They are an independent human rights organisation dedicated to the realisation of equal access to justice for all.

New Zealand

Equal Justice Project (equaljusticeproject.co.nz)

A student led initiative empowering communities to seek equal justice through education, service and advocacy. The Equal Justice Project aims to continue its mission of addressing issues of equity, redress and representation through four main projects: Pro Bono, Community, Communications and Access.

The Human Rights Foundation (humanrightsfoundation .wordpress.com)

An NGO promoting and defending human rights through research based education and advocacy. They make submissions on new laws with human rights implications while also monitoring compliance and implementation of New Zealand's international obligations in accordance with the requirements of the international conventions New Zealand has signed.

Poland

Academia Iuris Foundation (academiaiuris.pl)

This foundation provides free legal aid for those who cannot otherwise afford to pay. Under the supervision of professional consultants, law students help to solve legal problems. Their mission is to educate young lawyers and integrate the legal community around the idea of free legal aid for people.

The Halina Nieć Legal Aid Centre (pomocprawna.org/
wersja-angielska)
Their mission is to offer free legal aid for socially marginalised
people, whose rights and freedoms are violated; development
of democracy; promotion of the concept of respecting human
rights and the rule of law; shaping civil society and promoting
the culture of law in Poland.

Portugal
Pro Bono Portugal (probono.org.pt)
PBP's main goal is to achieve social cohesion by promoting
free legal assistance to individuals and other NGO's through
a network of legal professionals.

Romania
Equality and Human Rights Action Centre (actedo.org/en)
ACTEDO is a Romanian registered NGO which promotes
fundamental rights and gender equality and acts against
human rights violations. They aim to support vulnerable
groups to access justice by establishing a program of pro bono
legal assistance.

The Foundation for Civil Society Development (fdsc.ro/eng)
With the aim of being a powerful and influential civil society
advocate with responsible citizens involved, FCSD promotes
the interests and values for the benefit of communities. They
provide technical assistance, consulting and training, advocacy, information, research on high quality standards and aim
to increase the visibility of NGOs.

Spain

La Fundación más que Derecho (fundacionmasquederecho
.org)
Created with a strong commitment to society, and with the
aim to work to improve the areas that are closest to them,
such as study, training, dissemination and knowledge of laws,
especially those relating to Human Rights in all areas and at
all levels of society.

Hazloposible (hazloposible.org/en)
An organisation that works in innovative ways to boost participation from society in causes that benefit society. They
develop projects that channel capacity, talent, time and the
hope of thousands of people to NGO's that need collaboration
to support their causes. Through their website people choose
how they want to volunteer, and they allow organisations to
have a platform where they can publish their employment
offers and recruit the best professionals to give their talent to
social causes.

United Kingdom

LawWorks (lawworks.org.uk)
LawWorks is a charity which aims to provide free legal help
to individuals and community groups who cannot afford to
pay for it and who are unable to access legal aid.

The National Pro Bono Centre (nationalprobonocentre.org.uk)
A centre designed to be a 'hub' for pro bono charities across
the legal sector. It supports the wide range of pro bono projects

and brokerage which the charities support, helping individuals and community groups all over England and Wales.

United States
American Civil Liberties Union (aclu.org)
The ACLU aim to protect civil liberties through a nationwide network of staffed offices in every US state, Washington DC, and Puerto Rico. With more than 1.2 million members, nearly 300 staff attorneys and thousands of volunteer attorneys, the ACLU fights government abuses of individual freedoms including speech and religion, a woman's right to choose, the right to due process and a citizens' rights to privacy.

Appleseed (appleseednetwork.org)
With offices across the United States and Mexico, Appleseed enables lawyers to both volunteer their expertise to individuals in need of advice, and to work on broader social justice initiatives. They also provide training and technical assistance, particularly in communications, development, project management and board development. It was established by Ralph Nader and some of his classmates at Harvard Law School.

Equal Justice Works (equaljusticeworks.org)
The mission of Equal Justice Works is to create a just society by mobilising the next generation of lawyers committed to equal justice. To achieve this, they offer opportunities to law students and lawyers, providing training and skills that enable them to provide effective representation to underserved communities and causes.

Other pro bono services
International
Taproot Foundation (taprootfoundation.org)
This is the leading international pro bono organisation world-wide. It connects non-profits and social change organisations with passionate, skilled volunteers who share their expertise pro bono. Through their programs, business professionals deliver marketing, strategy, HR and IT solutions that organisations need to achieve their missions.

European Union
GROUPE SOS (groupe-sos.org)
For 30 years, GROUPE SOS has been putting economic value creation at the service of the interests of the general public. In so doing, it provides responses to the issues of today's society by developing innovative solutions in its five main fields of activity: youth, employment, health, solidarity and seniors. The founder, Jean-Marc Borrello, was one of the first social entrepreneurs in Europe and knows about The Good Lobby's work.

Australia
Resonate (highskillsvolunteering.com)
Resonate was established to narrow the gap between the corporate and community sectors by creating a shared value. They achieve this through the facilitation of workshops, group events and high-skills volunteering.

Canada

WorkInNonProfits.ca (workinnonprofits.ca/index)
Committed to helping build and strengthen Canada's non-profit sector, WorkInNonProfits.ca, connects non-profits across the country with job seekers as well as suppliers of services and products.

Endeavour (endeavourvolunteer.ca/)
Endeavour is dedicated to enabling non-profit organisations to improve and sustain their community impact. To achieve their mission, they are committed to providing volunteer consulting to non-profit organisations that otherwise may not be able to afford professional consulting services and engaging the community in providing volunteer consulting.

France

Pro Bono Lab (probonolab.org)
A lab that mobilises workers, students and professionals in search of work to help those organisations with a social purpose. It was founded by HEC alumni and friends Antoine Colonna d'Istria and Yoann Kassi-Viver.

Le Mouvement Des Entrepreneurs Sociaux (mouves.org)
The Movement of Social Entrepreneurs (Mouves) is a movement of people who want to volunteer and construct a humane economy which responds efficiently to the needs of society in employment, health, education and housing.

Passerelles et Compétences (passerellesetcompetences.org/pcsite)

An association recognising the public interest to volunteer, whose mission is to promote '*bénévolat de compétences*', a form of solidarity better suited to the competencies and availability of professionals. The founder is my friend Patrick Bertrand.

Germany

Proboneo (proboneo.de)

Proboneo brings committed professionals and managers together with social organisations so that good ideas can find professional support and experts can do something for themselves and for society. It was founded by my friend Claudia Leissner.

Poland

Fundacja Dobra Sieć (dobrasiec.org/en)

The Good Network Foundation is passionate about new technologies and convinced that they can help change the world for the better. The internet is a link between the most distant corners of the world, giving people the resources which they may not find in their environment.

United Kingdom

Reach (reachskills.org.uk)

Through their self-service platform, Reach promotes the benefits of skills-based volunteering, attracts prospective volunteers and encourages non-profits to engage skilled volunteers in their work. They enable professionals and non-profits to find their ideal volunteering match with the aim of radically increasing both the scale and impact of volunteering.

United States
Bayes Impact (bayesimpact.org)
As a technology non-profit their mission is to build the social services of the future. They leverage software and data science to deliver personalised and scalable interventions for millions of underserved people across the world.

Catchafire (catchafire.org)
The leading skills-based volunteering platform connecting high impact organisations in need with talented professionals eager to give back their skills. Through Catchafire's technology, pre-scoped project opportunities, and ongoing customer support, they provide meaningful, transformational volunteer experiences for every volunteer and organisation in the community. It was founded and led by my friend Rachel Chong.

Datakind (datakind.org)
Datakind brings together top data scientists with leading social change organisations to collaborate on cutting-edge analytics and advanced algorithms to maximize social impact. The pro bono data science innovation team tackle critical humanitarian issues in the fields of education, poverty, health, human rights, the environment and cities.

Pro Bono Net (probono.net)
An NGO dedicated to increasing access to justice through innovative uses of technology and increased volunteer lawyer participation.

The St. Bernard Project (sbpusa.org)
SBP was founded in March 2006 by Zack Rosenburg and Liz McCartney and is now, with the tremendous support of donors, volunteers and corporate partners, a national organisation, recognised as a leader in disaster resilience and recovery, whose mission is to shrink time between disaster and recovery.

The Washington Peace Center
(washingtonpeacecenter.org)
The Washington Peace Center provides education, resources and action for those working for positive social change and a world free from oppression. It is an anti-racist, grassroots, multi-issue organisation working for peace, justice and non-violent social change.

Pro bono marketing

Pimp My Cause (pimpmycause.org)
Pimp My Cause brings together worthwhile causes with talented marketers – including innovators, strategists, advertisers, graphic designers, web developers, PR specialists and researchers who can provide transformational input pro bono.

Movies to watch

All the President's Men (1976), directed by Alan J. Pakula

All the Way (2016), directed by Jay Roach

Battle in Seattle (2007), directed by Stuart Townsend

Bringing Down a Dictator (2002), directed by Steve York

The Brussels Business: Who Runs the European Union? (2012), directed by Matthieu Lietaert and Friedrich Moser

Chi-Raq (2015), directed by Spike Lee

The Corporation (2005), directed by Mark Achbar and Jennifer Abbott

Dr. Strangelove or: How I Learned to Stop Worrying and Love the Bomb (1964), directed by Stanley Kubrick

Fahrenheit 9/11 (2004), directed by Michael Moore

A Force More Powerful (1999), directed by Steve York

The Fourth World War (2003), directed by Richard Rowley

Good Night, and Good Luck (2005), directed by George Clooney

Manufacturing Consent: Noam Chomsky and the Media (1992), directed by Mark Achbar and Peter Wintonick

Milk (2008), directed by Gus Van Sant

The Most Dangerous Man in America: Daniel Ellsberg and the Pentagon Papers (2009), directed by Rick Goldsmith and Judith Ehrlich

Our Brand Is Crisis (2006), Rachel Boynton

Selma (2014), directed by Ava DuVernay

Thank You for Smoking (2005), directed by Jason Reitman

V For Vendetta (2005), directed by James McTeigue

Television series to watch

Alpha House (Amazon Studios), 2013–14

The Circus: Inside the Greatest Political Show on Earth (Showtime), 2016

The Good Wife (CBS), 2009–16

House of Cards (Netflix), 2013–present

John Adams (HBO), 2008

Political Animals (USA), 2012

Show Me a Hero (HBO), 2015

The West Wing (NBC), 1999–2006

Yes Minister! (BBC), 1980, 1984

Index

Index